Passionate Journey

Passionate Journey

The Spiritual Autobiography of
Satomi Myōdō

TRANSLATED & ANNOTATED BY
SALLIE B. KING

STATE UNIVERSITY OF NEW YORK PRESS

Published by
State University of New York Press, Albany

© 1993 State University of New York

For information, address State University of New York Press,
State University Plaza, Albany, N.Y., 12246

Production by Cathleen Collins
Marketing by Nancy Farrell

Library of Congress Cataloging in Publication Data

Satomi, Myōdō, 1896–1978.
Journey in search of the way : the spiritual autobiography of
Satomi, Myōdō / translated and annotated by Sallie B. King.
p. cm.
ISBN 0-7914-1971-1—ISBN 0-7914-1972-X (pbk.)
1. Satomi, Myōdō, 1896–1978. 2. Priests, Zen—Japan—Biography.
I. Title.
BQ984.A69947A3 1993
294.3'927'092—dc20
[B]   93-28484
                                                            CIP

10 9 8 7 6 5 4 3 2 1

FOR STEVE

Contents

~ CONTENTS ~

Preface

SATOMI MYŌDŌ'S *Journey in Search of the Way* is an autobiography, an account of a spiritual journey along several
religious paths, through delusion, mystery, insight, and realization. In her wandering, the author was often lost; as she
put it, "I tried a lot of absurd things." The desire to find
the Way, however, was strong; she continued her journey to
its end.

"Way" translates the Japanese *michi* (also pronounced *tō* or
dō in compounds). It is the same as the Chinese *Tao*. The Way is
two things at once. It is Truth or Reality, in the religious sense
of the way things ultimately are, the true nature of life and the
universe. It is also a path, a way of life that is in full harmony
with the true nature of things. For those who have not yet
found the Way, the path leads them to realize the Truth for
themselves, experientially; for those who have found it, the
path is a vehicle for expressing that knowledge, a way of living that is a natural and spontaneous manifestation of that
knowledge.

Of her search for the Way, Satomi-san says, "I journeyed
because I desired to find the Way of Truth, the Way which
could put an end to all suffering." One who knows the Truth,
the Way, will no longer suffer, for one who knows the Way can
no longer be at odds with life. To know the Way is to see the
"big picture," to see life, change, time, existence as they are in
themselves, not through the eyes of a frightened being re-

sentful of infirmity, death, and the other vicissitudes of life. To know the Way is to know life and to know oneself as an individual at home in the cosmos. It is to see one's rightful position in life, one's belongingness, not in a self-centered way, but in a way in which the infinite interrelationships of oneself and all other beings in the cosmos—both animate and inanimate—are made clear. Becoming free of egotism, one who knows the Way sees things the way they are, rather than how she or he might wish they were. Thus one no longer struggles in vain against the inevitabilities of life, but accepts whatever life may bring, with a calm and peaceful heart. Thus, to know the Way is to be free of care, free of suffering, and to live in a truthful, sincere, and harmonious manner.

In Japanese culture, there are many ways, or paths, to discover or express the Way. One of the distinctive features of Japanese culture is the abundance of traditional arts, crafts, and religious disciplines, determined practice of any of which is said to lead to realization of the Way. The martial arts fall into this category—jūdō, aikidō, kendō (the way of the sword)—as do bushidō (the way of the warrior), shodō (calligraphy), chadō (the way of Tea), shidō (the way of poetry), and many other arts. Among religious traditions, Zen Buddhism is directly equated with the Way by its adherents; the Japanese national religious tradition, Shinto, the Way of the gods, ultimately hopes to bring humanity into harmony with the gods. The Way, then, may appear to take many forms. All of these, however, are felt to be expressive of a single reality, a reality best demonstrated not in terms of creed or doctrine, of which all these traditions are shy, but in the actions and life of one who knows. This book is the record of the life and thought of a Japanese woman who sought such a Way.

~ PREFACE ~

There are two major sections to this book: the translation of Satomi-san's autobiography and my commentary on the auto-biography. Though the commentary frequently refers to the autobiography, each part can be read independently of the other. Thus the reader may choose to read the autobiography first; the notes to the text should be adequate to clarify un-familiar terms, and the commentary could be read afterward to deepen the reader's understanding. Alternatively, the reader may prefer to read the commentary first as an introduction that elucidates the philosophical and religious ideas and practices as well as the historical context of Satomi-san's story and thus enriches the reading of the autobiography. The commentary can also serve as a brief introduction to popular Japanese reli-gion in the modern period; the autobiography then, literally, brings this discussion to life.

Acknowledgments

FIRST THANKS must go to *Kahawai: Journal of Women and Zen* and its former co-editor, Susan Murcott, who introduced me to Satomi-san's manuscript and arranged contacts necessary for the translation to proceed. I am grateful to Yamada Kōun Rōshi, president of the lay Buddhist organization Sambōkyōdan, for permission to translate this text, which first appeared in its journal, *Kyōshō*. Yamada Rōshi took time out of his busy schedule to discuss with me his own personal knowledge of Satomi-san. Roshi Robert Aitken of Hawaii introduced me to the Japanese Zen circle that I needed to meet and also wrote a remembrance of Satomi-san, parts of which I have incorporated into the Epilogue.

Sincere thanks to several of Satomi-san's friends with whom I was able to speak in Japan: Shimomura Mitsuko, who remarked on the deep impression Satomi-san had made on her and also encouraged the project in tangible ways; Igarashi Kazuo, a very close friend from both Tokyo and Hokkaido days; and Miyazaki-san, the group's historian, all of whom shared their personal knowledge of Satomi-san in vivid anecdotes and fond memories. Thanks likewise to Satomi-san's daughter Satomi Kuniko, who not only welcomed me into her home for an evening of discussion, but also searched through her belongings for pictures and mementos of her mother and personally escorted me up the hill to the "sacred site" Satomi-san had established across from the Satomi home.

A number of scholars greatly helped me in understanding some of the particulars of Satomi-san's story. Akiba Yutaka checked the translation against the original. Anne-Marie Bouchy met with me on a number of occasions to discuss the *miko* and introduce me to the world of practicing *miko*. Maggie Childs, my colleague at Southern Illinois University, read through the translation. Gorai Shigeru spoke with me about popular Japanese religion and Shinto. Minoru Kiyota gave me encouragement and many useful suggestions, and clarified for me several points in Buddhist thought that were used in odd ways in the text. Nagao Gadjin explained a number of Buddhist technical terms and usages, and also personally traced an exceedingly obscure reference for me. Yanagida Seizan discussed with me at length the Zen figures, sayings, and ideas that appear in the text and also shared with me his thoughts on the relationship between philosophy and practice in Zen. Finally, special thanks to Helen Hardacre, who not only discussed with me both the general plan of this work and various details of prewar Japanese religion, but also made time to read through the Commentary. Her comments, corrections, and suggestions were a great boon. I am very grateful to her for sharing her vast knowledge of Japanese religion with me.

From the world of religious practitioners, I must mention the staff of Iso no Kami Jingū in Tenri City, who discussed with me *chinkon* practices similar to those described by Satomi-san. I am especially indebted to Nakai Shigeno, a *miko* who several times allowed me to observe her at work and discussed in a straightforward manner her life as a *miko*. I very much appreciate the time and insight shared with me by all these very busy people.

While in Japan, I made use of the library facilities made available to me by a number of universities. Thanks in this regard to Kyoto University, Dōshisha University, and Tenri

University, the Institute for Zen Studies of Hanazono College, and the National Council of Churches Center for the Study of Japanese Religions.

For financial support, my greatest debt is to the Japan Foundation, which provided me with a 1983–1984 Professional Fellowship enabling me to travel to Japan, finish the manuscript, and, most important, speak with all the people in Japan who shared personal and professional information unavailable, for the most part, anywhere else. The staff of the Japan Foundation also provided important support. Thanks to the Office of Research Development and Administration and the International Education Office at Southern Illinois University, which provided additional support, and to the Department of Philosophy at SIU for allowing me to take leave after having joined the faculty only five months earlier.

My debts to all these persons and institutions are many. Thanks to all for help without which this project could not have been completed. Responsibility for what has been written, however, is mine alone.

More personal thanks to three people. Mayumi and Makio Morikawa, our neighbors in Japan, helped in countless ways, both professionally and personally. Not only did they help us establish ourselves materially in our arrangements with landlady, banker, shopkeepers, doctors, and others, but they also shared emotionally and intellectually in the encouragement and furtherance of the present work. It is impossible to recount here everything they did for us from the day of our arrival in Kyoto until the very moment we left, as they helped us to the train station with our staggering load of baggage.

Finally, I would like to publicly thank my husband, Steve, who read through the translation and suggested needed improvements, who discussed the manuscript with me again and again as I worked through it, and who has constantly encouraged and supported me over the years in all my efforts. It is common in our world—in Japan, in the United States, and elsewhere—for wives to put their interests aside for the sake of their husbands. It is rare indeed for a husband to do the same for his wife. Throughout our marriage, Steve has always been willing to put himself second for my sake. On this occasion, he readily set aside his own studies and interests to travel to Japan with me and care for our baby daughter while I worked. It is vividly clear to me that the many hours I spent in libraries or speaking with scholars, friends of Satomi-san, and religious practitioners would not have been possible without this gift. It is also clear that such behavior is a gift; it is not to be requested, much less expected and taken for granted. Would that such self-sacrifice on the part of women everywhere for the sake of their husbands be recognized for the gift that it is. Here I can only thank my husband.

PART ONE

The Spiritual Autobiography of Satomi Myōdō

I

Moral Education

I WAS BORN in the twenty-ninth year of the Meiji era (1896). This year, 1956, I am an old nun of sixty years. For forty years I wandered in search of the Way. And though in this time I traveled about, visited teachers, and received many kinds of instruction, I was by no means able to attain the final peace; the cares of life still troubled me. What I wanted was the Way of Truth, the Way capable of ending all suffering.

Thus I came to Tokyo and, through a wonderful karmic link,[1] came to receive instruction at Taiheiji Temple; what's more, I received the guidance of Yasutani Rōshi. Every month I was permitted to attend *sesshin*[2] at Shinkōji Temple in Saitama Prefecture. At the second *sesshin*, I am happy to say, I obtained the real essence of Buddhism; that is, I realized that to which the living Buddha's teachings refer. Though I say this, I don't mean that I realized the great, broad, deep, and far-reaching Truth in its entirety. I just realized a part of it—I found the door leading inside. But in that moment of realization, that which had been bound up inside me for many years was suddenly and completely released. As in the parable of the rich man and his destitute son,[3] in which the son wanders about for years before returning home, I too have now finally struggled back to the door of my home. I am happy that I can now take the first step in practicing real Buddhism. I am infinitely grateful. In my inadequate way, I would like to write a little now

3

about my meager experience. Please excuse the objectionable passages. I will begin with what motivated me to seek the Way.

When I was young—until the age of twenty or so—I was no good at all. I was a real devil! Why was I like that? Of course this was the result of my karma, but what additionally spurred on that bad karma was, first and foremost, the contradiction between my elementary school's curriculum in ethics and the everyday life of the adults around me. During ethics period in school we were made to listen to all sorts of lectures in "moral education" and were prevailed upon to "be good" and "tell the truth," and so on. When I went home, however, I found lies and deception. One moment a guest would arrive and my parents would say sweet words to his face and play up to him, but when he left, instantly, like a hand turning over, they would bad-mouth and ridicule him. Such events were not unusual. I wondered if this went on only in my home; but no, whatever home, whatever adult—even my respected schoolteacher— all were the same. I didn't know what to make of it. "What is this all about?" I asked myself. "Oh, I get it! As a subject of study, the morality we learn in school is best just drummed into the head, like a recording. But life and morality are two abso-lutely different things. The reality of everyday life is built on lies." It got to the point where the question of truth and falsehood ceased to enter my mind. This was my elementary school period.

With these attitudes, I entered Girls' High School. I went to the Public Girls' School, which took as its motto "Good Wives and Wise Mothers."[4] Every Monday morning the principal would assemble all the students in the auditorium and give a talk. It was always bound to be scrupulous and exhaustive instruction for the benefit of the future good wives and wise mothers. At the conclusion of the talk he invariably added a word of advice: be careful with members of the opposite sex. According to this advice, the male of the species is nothing but a fearful wild beast with gnashing fangs that will swoop down upon any young girl he fancies. How could a girl concerned with her future prospects sacrifice herself to this beast? Don't be careless! Don't go near them! Don't look them in the face! Such were his stern words. He would then give some concrete examples. I was subjected to these lectures every week for four years until graduation. The aim of this grandmotherly kindness was to cultivate the flawless good wife and wise mother and to preserve her virginal innocence until marriage. In my case, however, things turned out just the opposite.

I absolutely couldn't stand men! A man to me was some kind of disgusting jet-black panther. What was marriage? What was a good wife and wise mother? Wasn't she the prey of that despicable panther? Was there ever such a contradiction? Was there ever a speech so degrading to us? Was he saying that right now men were like wild animals to us, but that later—when we married—they would become blessed, godlike beings on whom we should rely? How absurd! I felt very indignant toward the principal's speeches. At the same time, a fierce resentment blazed up in me toward "them"—those beasts who gobbled up the pure virgins. I was especially disgusted with charming men; I imagined that their charm would cause even greater injury to the virgins. I cursed those men as the bitterest enemy: "I put the evil eye on you! I wish you would drop dead!" My heart's desire was to directly approach this dreadful beast, twist him around my little finger, and toss him over my shoulder. I wanted to deliver a shattering blow.

At that time, my life revolved around the world of literature. After graduation from Girls' High School, I went to Tokyo, dreaming of becoming a writer. I stayed at my uncle's house and became the student of a certain novelist who was famous at

5

the time. But my feelings toward men had not changed. I selected a target, devised a plan of attack, and steadily began to carry it out. My chances of victory were quite good, I thought. "He's bound to fall for it!" I told myself, thinking it would be easy for me to knock him speechless. I had faith in myself.

But what a mistake! At the critical moment, *bang!* the bottom fell through. The one whose luck gave out was not he but I: I got pregnant. At that time, unlike now, abortion was a terrible thing. I was afraid of being punished if I had one. My future prospects were pitch black. What could I do? I didn't want to hold on to him just to finish him off. Since things had turned out like this, I no longer cared about his state of mind. He was in love with me, but that was not at issue for me. It was unnecessary even to think of marriage.

My studies meant a lot to me. But I was pregnant. I returned to my parents' home, alone and without purpose. My parents were poor farmers in a mountain village in Hokkaido. I was an only child. My parents' sole desire was to make something of me, with their limited means. To do this, they had sent me to an exclusive girls' school and had even gone so far as to send me to Tokyo to advance their desire. But this parental love had never once gotten through to me and touched my heart.

Meanwhile, I just grew more and more fretful. But since in this case I certainly reaped what I had sowed, I couldn't complain. My parents seemed to have vague suspicions about my extraordinary bodily condition but deliberately avoided referring to it. I wanted to be severely scolded, condemned and thrown out, or told to go kill myself. But I was going to have to be the one to bring the subject up, somehow or other. I too kept silent.

Every day the three of us silently arose, and silently we went to work in the fields. As for me—with my body, which couldn't be more shameful, and my face, which one could hardly bear to look at—I just wanted to crawl into a hole and disappear. Looking like a barrel whose hoops were about to burst, and in a condition of utter despair, I was incapable even of dying. I could do nothing but sit back and watch my shame grow. I felt wretched, miserable, ashen—as if I were traveling alone at night through an endless wilderness, wearily dragging one foot after the other.

One day I went as usual to the fields, working and getting covered with dirt. From a distance, my father urgently called my name. I went to see what he wanted and found Father squatting at the edge of the field, gazing intently at something. A moment passed. I felt a little strange squatting quietly by my father's side. Absently, my eye caught his line of vision. There was nothing but a single weed growing there. Softly, Father began to speak.

"I've been watching this for some time . . . it's quite inter- esting. . . . Look! A winged ant is crawling up the weed. It climbs up, little by little . . . it seems to want to reach the top. Oh, it fell! There—it's climbing again! For some time now it's been doing this over and over again." Just as he said, a winged ant was climbing up the weed and falling, falling and climbing up again.

"Here! Climbing again! Look, it must be tired now. When it's tired, it stretches its legs and beats its little wings up and down like that. That's how it restores its energy. Then, when it's rested, it starts climbing again."

Father continued to speak without taking his eyes off the brave little insect. I too inadvertently became intrigued. I stared at it intently for quite a while. Suddenly, it hit me—I understood what my father was getting at! It was unbearable! I quickly got up and left his side. I ran to the shady side of the field where no one could see me and fell down wailing. I cried and cried in anguish.

"Oh, Father, I understand; I really understand! Do you love me so much? I'm so unfilial![5] Do you still cherish such hope for me, when I am so disgusted with myself? How unworthy I am! But how grateful! I'm sorry! Oh, Father, from now on I promise to be a filial daughter! I promise to make you happy!" I determined to repay my father's love, no matter what. Just then, an iron shackle was broken and at once a broad expanse of light burst upon the world.

2

Sincerity

I HAD NEVER KNOWN such a wonderful world as the one I experienced in that moment. I saw the grass and trees, the hills, river, fields, and stones, the hoe and sickle, the birds and dogs, the roofs and windows—all shining brightly under the same sun. For me it was a wonderful breath of fresh air. Both the animate and the inanimate were vividly alive, familiarly addressing me and waving their hands. Struck by the unearthly exquisiteness of this world, I broke into tears and lifted up my face, weeping, in ecstasy. I saw right through myself and completely emptied my bag of emotional problems. All those words about morality that I had heard at elementary school, and that I had thought were just lectures to be forgotten, suddenly took on the form of living truth for me.

"So there is such a thing as sincerity after all. There is a world of truth. Now that Father's sincerity has touched me, I understand what it is. What a lucky person I am! I've found sincerity! I've found the lost jewel!" With warm tears flowing freely, I gained the sure and unshakable conviction that "at the bottom of all things is sincerity." I felt as if I had gained a million friends.

As I looked back at the mass of immorality I had been, I saw what a gloomy and anxious state of being it was. I couldn't help pitying those who had not yet awakened to sincerity. What a miserable way to live! Somehow or other, I felt, those people must be made to comprehend sincerity. Somehow or other, they must be drawn into its realm. Thus I immediately resolved, "From now on I will dive right into the midst of those people, maintaining sincerity to the end. I'll even die for their sake!"

I was prepared to meet rejection. Ridicule, misunderstanding, abuse, even physical attack—did any of it matter? My mind was made up. "Even into a blazing fire, brandishing the single word *sincerity*—onward!" I believed without a doubt that sincerity could raise the dead. I danced with joy! I felt like running around in circles, shouting, "There is such a thing as sincerity! Honestly there is! Please believe me! I beg you!" But could I get people to believe me?

Certainly there was such a thing as sincerity. I believed in it. "But what is sincerity? What is its true nature?" I asked myself. Though it was faint-hearted of me, I knew I couldn't give a definite answer to the question. "I'm no good at that kind of thing. For that you need someone who has mastered the Way and penetrated sincerity. Such a person can give a satisfactory answer to anyone," I thought. To clarify the true nature of sincerity would be the first step in my search for the Way.

I realized that until this time I had been impure and cold-hearted. I had never shed so much as one tear for truth. I had never thought of others nor felt the need to do so. Self-centered and capricious, I had thought I could play with others in any way I wanted. I had thought "honest person" was another term for "great fool." I had cherished the superiority complex of an evil person. I was haughty, but in truth I was an insignificant nobody. The moment I was struck by my father's sincerity, though, I truly turned around 180 degrees.

I gave birth to my elder daughter in December of the year I returned home. The baby's father had come to my home about two months before. The son of a Hokkaido stationmaster, he had gone to Tokyo to study but quit school to come live with me. He was a handsome man, steadfast and pure-hearted. My parents immediately announced the wedding party and invited the people of the village.

My husband did all sorts of unfamiliar work—chopping wood, caring for horses, anything and everything. The next year I gave birth to my second daughter. But even though I was the mother of two children, I didn't feel like a wife to him, and the husband-wife love never developed. I did not want to get a divorce, though. Why? For the sake of the children. I couldn't burden the innocent children with the unhappiness brought on by my immorality. I felt there could be no excuse for making them orphans,[1] come what may. The atmosphere at home, however, began to move in the opposite direction of these intentions. A chasm was gradually opening up between my husband and my parents. I was in a predicament. If I spoke, I would make the bad feelings between the two sides worse. So I held my peace. Finally, one night, my father and my husband quarreled over an insignificant thing. In the end, my husband stormed out of the house in the middle of the night.

I lived on with my parents in our Hokkaido mountain village, gathering firewood and cultivating the fields. Until now my mental energy had been dissipated in the delusory condition of the sixth consciousness.[2] But starting from the time my husband left and lasting for about two years, my mental condition was in a very strange spiritual stage. Was it some kind of bizarre mysticism? Was it lunacy? Often, while remaining in this same body, I leaped over the world of humanity and ascended to the distant world of beginningless eternity. There I was completely enfolded in the heart of God. I lost my form and became one with God, the solitary Light, which peacefully, truly peacefully, shone out all around. It was indescribable, blissful fulfillment. This condition progressed until I stumbled into the world of absolute nothingness and lapsed into unconsciousness. From this state I again advanced until hallucinations began to appear.

3

My Strange
Mental Condition

MY FIRST HALLUCINATION occurred right after the children's father left me. It was a day in late spring. I say "late spring," but this was the north country and, moreover, a village deep in the mountains. The cuckoo had finally begun to sing and the farmers breathed a sigh of relief, as that was the signal that the last frost had passed. It was planting season. I went, as usual, into the fields. I worked alone.

As I gazed out over the broad expanse of gently sloping mountain fields, brilliant flecks of sunlight sparkled like scattered gold dust. Heat waves shimmered from the surface of the freshly plowed mounds of earth. I had finished a section of the work and was rather tired, so I sat down on a pile of chaff between the fields. In an instant, before I knew what hit me, I fell into a trance.

I don't know how much time passed then, but suddenly, from out of nowhere, I heard a grave voice calling out my name, "Matsuno! Matsuno!" [1] I blinked my eyes open and again heard the voice, saying, "Look over there!" I peered over suspiciously, and . . . how strange! A moment ago a field of plain dirt had been there, but now the field was bursting with peas in full bloom. I looked more closely and . . . what?! The pea field was crawling with green caterpillars. The rustling sound they made as they devoured the leaves, stems, and flowers made me choke.

"The human world is decimated like this, too!" This was simultaneously the message of the voice and my own intuition.

Then *pop!* in an instant the pea field vanished and the place became a dense forest.

"Huh?" I wondered for an instant.

"The roots are already cut"—that voice again! I strained my ears. . . . "The roots of the rampant evil of this world are already cut in the invisible world. Matsuno, stand up and fight!" This was the stern command.[2]

"I will!" I vowed. "I'll just have to give a push and that'll finish it off!" I danced for joy with my sense of mission. In that moment, I returned to my usual self. The vision vanished; the voice ceased. But the psychological effect continued vividly, guiding me forcibly and casting a definite hue over every aspect of my daily life.

My mind was abnormally strained. I felt a thrill of adventure in embracing this "sacred mystery," as if I were soaring to the peak of a distant, towering mountain. The "sacred mystery" was the "vow to the kami"[3] which I must not betray. I felt that if so much as one word of this leaked out, the demonic powers would instantly profit, the vow would lose all efficacy, and I would plunge headlong into hell!

From then on, I kept seeing these visions and dreams, and at the same time I became so impatient to carry out my vow that I couldn't keep still. I burned with the feeling that I must soon go to Tokyo to proceed with my sworn objective. But I could not formulate a concrete plan to accomplish it.

I came to wonder whether I really needed such a plan. "Anything would be all right; the important thing is to get going. Strike out! Forward! Hup, two, three, four! That's the way! No need to worry about the next moment, just press ahead! Step by step, hurling myself against all obstacles!"

One day I stood before my father and mother and made a formal request. "Please send me to Tokyo again." This was three months after my husband had left home.

"What do you want to do in Tokyo?"

"Study."

"Studying is fine, but what on earth would you study?"

"I can't say."

"Why not?"

I kept silent. I couldn't tell anyone. The divine secret must not be revealed!

My mother burst out, "You probably want to go to your husband's place. Well, that's understandable—"

Father broke in, "Well, if you want to go, all right, but I—"

"No, it's not that," I cut him off. I knew what he was going to say. I appreciated his grandmotherly heart, but what was that to the new me?

I advanced one step: "Really, it's selfish, but I'd like to ask you to take care of the children for a little while."

Both parents stared at me in bewilderment for a moment, and then Father asked, "You want to leave both children with us?"

"Yes! Please, will you?"

"We can't do it. Take one along with you!" Father quickly replied.

I was defeated. "All right." There was nothing I could do about it, I thought. "Well, I have one more request." I rallied myself for my second approach.

"Go ahead."

"I need about a hundred yen." This took death-defying courage.

"What would you do with a hundred yen? Thirty yen is plenty. I'll give you that, all right?"

"All right." There was nothing I could do about that either.

Thus, with a nursing child on my back and thirty yen in my pocket, I left immediately for Tokyo. I say thirty yen, but the thirty yen of that day was worth more than ten thousand of today's yen.[4] Anyway, for less than five yen, I was able to go from Sapporo to Ueno Station, Tokyo.

4

I Lose My Baby

AS SOON AS I arrived at Ueno Station, I scoured the newspaper ads to find room and board. By day's end, I had moved into a place over a newspaper shop in Koishikawa[1] and found work as an evening newspaper saleswoman. The landlady was a kind woman, single and over fifty. I also worked at selling *nattō*[2] in the early mornings. Thus, whatever else happened, my life was stabilized.

The following year Tōyo University started a program in the philosophy of religion and I was able to attend the lectures. I left the baby sleeping alone in the apartment while I was at school. When I returned, her face was always wrinkled from tears and her bottom soaked with urine. I cried and thought, "We'll have to endure each other for a while." At this time, my milk began to dry up because of overwork. Since the baby was hungry, she cried throughout the night, and as a result I couldn't sleep either. I was dead tired, and at school I would even doze off during lectures.

On top of this, something happened that gave me a great shock. My husband's aunt, who lived in Tokyo, saw me with the baby on my back one day from a streetcar. This caused an uproar, and in the end the parents from both sides came to Tokyo. In my apartment above the newspaper store, they collided head-on, arguing over the baby and me. On my husband's side were his mother, the aunt, and my husband himself. On my side were my father and the landlady.

My mother-in-law was built solidly like a man, and her words, too, were solid and sensible. She spoke earnestly and emotionally. Making her point, she closed in on my father. In response, my father's determination hardened and he insisted on a separation.

At the end of the day, neither side had won. My mother-in-law grilled me, "Don't you love the child?"

Then the landlady drew close to me and expressed her feelings: "You know, don't you, how much your father worries about you?"

I bit my lip and kept silent. Suddenly, my mother-in-law cried, "What kind of a demon is this mother?" She stood up and snatched the baby from my lap. I clung to my child, all confused. My husband jumped up and knocked me down. "It's no use with such a beast!" The three stormed out of the room, clutching the baby tightly.

"My darling baby! My poor baby! Why do I have to lose my baby? Why shouldn't I be able to love that baby the way my father loves me?" Finding myself suddenly overpowered like this, I lost my voice in sobs. Hot tears ran uncontrollably down my cheeks.

"Don't cry," Father tried to console me. "The child will be better off with them than living with you like this." But what did "better off" mean? What was really good for a nursing child? My heart ached. The landlady tried to comfort and encourage me, to make me resign myself, saying, "Now you're free. Now you can study in earnest," and so forth. But what good were all her words? They just made me want to cry. I didn't want to hear anything she said. I felt that I would faint.

But I recovered my spirits as I recalled that time in the fields. Hadn't I vowed deeply in my heart that to repay Father's love I would gladly suffer any hardship? I loved my child, but shouldn't I love my father still more? I clenched my teeth with determination.

I looked directly in my father's face. "Father, please forgive me! I haven't forgotten. Oh, Father! Please set your mind to rest. I won't do anything else to worry you."

The next day Father gave his heartfelt thanks to the landlady, entrusted me to her care, and finally, with a peaceful look on his face, returned home.

Like a faintly flickering lamp that is finally consumed, my energy was completely exhausted when my father left. I didn't have the strength to do anything. Even though I felt there was no excuse for treating the landlady so rudely, all day long I pulled the futon quilt over my head and cried. I felt desolate without the baby sleeping in my arms. The child whom I had once felt to be a burden had really been the motivating force behind all my activities. It was precisely because the baby was there that I had been able to conquer all obstacles and press forward like a hero. Even my love for my father, even the strength of the oath to which my life was sacrificed, couldn't match the strength with which the baby had held my breast.

Unable to bear it, I would rise from bed like a sleepwalker and wander around outside, letting my faltering feet lead me where they would. When I came to my senses, I was always standing in front of that aunt's house in Kanda,[3] where my husband used to live. Wondering if the child was there, I would sneak around to the back and then to the front, like a thief. I would peek through a gap in the door and look around. Then, always disheartened, I would trudge back home. There was no reason to assume that either the baby or the others would be at this aunt's house. Although I knew this, I couldn't let it be without repeating it over and over like a daily lesson.

Thoughts of my father and of my vow to the kami jumped

about in my mind, taking on a variety of forms. But I was certainly hardest hit by the problem of the baby—there my thoughts were completely smashed into tiny fragments, and I couldn't make sense of anything. Surely the child cried for my breast. It broke my heart to think of it. I wrote a poem at that time:

> This mother is worse than a demon.
> If I die of insanity
> Don't grieve, my Sumiko.

Built up and torn down; built up and broken down. The rubble of Sai-no-Kawara[4] rattled around in my head and would give me no peace.

5

Complete Nervous Breakdown

It WAS SEVERAL MONTHS LATER, a snowy February night. As I lay on my bed between sleeping and waking, my mind drifted off to a garden with alpine flowers in bloom, the likes of which I had never seen. In a little while, a lacquer-black darkness seemed to fall like a curtain before my eyes. In the midst of this darkness, a huge, round, blood-red flower suddenly burst open. It looked like fireworks bursting in the sky. Just then my whole body was seized by a violent and uncontrollable trembling.

Suddenly, in my delirium, I saw a sword in the ceiling just above where I was lying. It was pointing down at me, piercing through the ceiling boards as if it would drop right onto my windpipe. I saw it as if I were looking through a pane of glass. "It's there to kill me," I thought. "It's the landlady. There's something evil about her. She thinks I suspect something and is afraid I'll expose her. She's scheming with her accomplice to do away with me! But the kami will stand by me! I have nothing to fear! I'll fix them—I'll get the jump on them!"

I got up quietly and slipped my coat on over my nightgown. Thus dressed, I escaped from the house through the second-floor window, running from roof to roof. I walked briskly away, letting my bare feet guide me. I was not cold nor was I even chilled. I finally reached a place that I thought was a beach. As I gazed out over the dark surface of the ocean, my thoughts ran like this: "I've got to cross the ocean and get to the Kegon Waterfall at Nikkō. In the pool below the waterfall, someone is crying out, 'Life is incomprehensible!' It's the young philosopher Fujimura Misao![1] He has thrown himself into the water and he hasn't come up yet! I'll jump in and save him!" When, as I believed, I did so, he floated lightly to the surface, though he had been down there a long time.

Suddenly, a voice cried, "Hallooo!"

"Yah! It's the accomplice! The rat!" I was frightened and tried to run away, but that guy grabbed the sleeve of my coat. Spinning around, I slipped out of the coat, leaving it in his hand, and ran away. He chased after me again and grabbed my nightgown. Once more I spun around and left him holding it.[2] Wearing just my underpants, I dashed away as fast as I could. From here and there people came running and surrounded me. I looked and saw that they were all policemen. It was the dead of night. I spent that night in a detention cell and was carried forcibly the next morning in a rickshaw to a mental hospital. I had finally gone insane.

> When I speak
> My lips are cold.
> The autumn wind.[3]

This is exactly how I felt. I often just babbled away, but when I did, I soon felt remorseful. "What kind of a fool am I? Just a shallow, affected dolt. From now on, I absolutely will not talk nonsense. My lips are sealed!" Thus I resolved and engraved the words upon my heart. But soon I was babbling again. I was a deeply troubled person. This was my journey in search of the

Way: feeling remorse, hating myself, and babbling nonsense. Please overlook all this.

At the mental hospital, I was first put into something that looked like a wild-animal cage, with thick steel bars. They threw me in there as if I were a lion. From time to time I would roar, "I have two minds in one body!"

The feeling came over me that I was in a trap made by evil people, but that I had to walk right into the danger with my eyes wide open and give myself up to it. The people around me all looked evil. I firmly believed that I alone was good. From this belief came a tremendous physical strength which filled my body with energy. I was afraid of nothing. "Try and kill me if you can! I'll never die!" I thought.

Suddenly, from beneath the corner edge of the cell, two or three flickers of bright red flame darted up, like the tongue of a snake. I saw the flame, in my hallucination, burning more and more fiercely. "The cell is burning up! Ah! Heaven comes to the rescue of good people! It's the plan of the highest kami for getting me out of here. Thank you! I will just be quiet and keep calm. I'll obey instructions from moment to moment, and everything will be fine."

Dawn came. Two or three people passed by the cell and peered in. Finally the nurse came and thrust a medicine bottle through the bars. "It's poison!" I said, knocking it abruptly out of her hand. I was thinking, "You can't fool me that way!" She unconcernedly picked it up and retreated, her slippers flapping with a *pat-pat-pat* down the hall.

The next day I was allowed to leave the cell and was moved to a large, open room. In this room were seventeen or eighteen female patients, each one behaving in an utterly self-absorbed manner. Some cried, some laughed, some grumbled. Some wandered restlessly to and fro. Some wore an apronlike garment that kept them from using their hands. They were screaming. I observed, though, that in this circle of comrades there were never any quarrels.

"These people are not insane," I thought. "Evil people trumped up this pretext of insanity for their own purposes and falsely confined these women here. The real meaning of their so-called insanity is the unknown danger they face from those evil people. It's a plot. The doctors here have been bought, those big nothings. They're going to slowly poison us."

Several days later I suddenly felt, "The people in this room are a little strange, aren't they?" There was a wrinkled old woman there, always sitting primly in her brightly colored kimono. I asked her how old she was.

"Sixteen," she said in a young girl's coquettish voice.

"Stranger and stranger," I thought.

Very shortly, I was moved to yet another room. Here there were about twenty people, all working diligently at making paper bags. I also was made to do this. The wages were settled up once a week, and with them one could buy whatever one wanted. I gradually came to enjoy this hospital life.

At that time, I began to perform in a play inside the hospital. I mingled daily with sane people in rehearsals, and some male patients as well.

"You'll be able to leave the hospital soon," one of the room's elder patients said to me enviously. "People who perform in the shows always leave the hospital."

"How awful! I'd like to stay here forever," I responded from my heart.

One day the nurse came to summon me, saying I had a visitor. When I entered the reception room, I was surprised to see my father standing there alone. He had come all the way from Hokkaido to pick me up. For a moment I was startled and at a loss: must I leave this pleasant hospital and return to the world of corruption? The painful memories of the past that I had utterly forgotten came flooding back all at once. "What an evil woman I am. I abandon my children, separate from my husband, and cause my parents such worry. . . . Was my first insight into sincerity wrong somehow? Was I deluded? What on earth is karma anyway?" Thinking such thoughts, I put my beloved hospital behind me and walked out with my father.

Father abruptly asked, "Well, what do you want to do now?" I had no idea. Unlike before, my mind was all foggy and indecisive. For now, at least, I had no desire to go to school. I suddenly remembered an uncle named Tetsumei on my father's side who was chief priest at a temple in Hakodate.

"Please send me to Tetsumei's."

"Nonsense." Father would not hear of it. He said, as if to himself, "It's no good taking her back to Hokkaido. Maybe I should talk it over with Gotō-san." Gotō-san was the landlady at the newspaper shop.

Gotō-san spoke kindly. "I have an acquaintance who is a master of physiognomy. Go see him and you'll be able to settle on a good plan."

I was soon taken to the home of this so-called master by Gotō-san. He gave this appraisal: "By nature, this woman is extremely imitative; therefore, if she were to be an actress, she would certainly succeed. Within that field, if she were to be a *kageki*[4] actress, her success would be all the greater."

Gotō-san made up her mind quickly. "Any occupation would do; if you could even be a success, it would be wonderful. If you were successful, you'd make your father very happy. If you were to go to school or something, it would take a long time, and who knows whether or not you would succeed. Why not become an actress instead?"

Father, too, was inclined to go along with this. I was reluctant, but I couldn't help being moved by his ardent parental love and his desire to help me. For me to succeed according to his desire—even if only for a while—would make him happy, and this I wanted very much. "To be sincere is to forget myself and serve others, to abandon all of my own desires and fulfill my father's expectations." Thus I admonished myself.

6

Kageki Actress

FOR A CONGRATULATORY GIFT, Gotō-san gave me a gorgeous kimono set as a first step toward a brilliant career. My father was delighted. As Gotō-san helped me put it on, he said, "You've probably never worn such a pretty kimono in your whole life." I was all choked up.

Two years later, I somehow managed to get a minor starring role to perform. This stage life seemed meaningless to me, though. Not only did it fail to raise any deep emotions within me, but it also could not appease my loneliness, which grew stronger day by day. I wondered what would come of such a life. Finally, unable to endure it any longer, I called on the actress who was the head of the troupe. I told her, "Every day we put our whole heart and soul into performing these plays, but do the plays do anybody any good?"

"What a fool you are! With these things, anything goes. If you can sell your name, that's good enough!"

I asked the same question of her husband, the troupe's manager. He replied, "Sure, they do plenty of good. First of all, plays can really inspire people."

"But it seems kind of tedious to me. I want to rescue people who are drowning right now in front of my eyes—"

He cut me off. "When such people see a play, it changes their whole outlook, and they're helped."

"But what about people who can't go see plays?"

27

"What a dummy! What's the matter with you? At any rate, you give it your all, and then you go that one step farther. . . . You've gradually become popular, haven't you?"

I remained silent.

"And what good is popularity? you ask. So what if the audience cheers you, right? You're upset because you can't save some kitten by the side of the road, right?"

I felt tears running down my face. "No good! Being an actress is no good for me! I still want to jump in and directly help a drowning person!"

In those days there was a gang called "Peragoro"[1] attached to the *kageki* troupe. Most of them were adolescents, young people who affected competence as actors. There was also a scoundrel of an old man, with obnoxious habits. Members of the gang were always going in and out of the dressing rooms and stealing the actresses' handkerchiefs, jewelry, and other things. They listened to whatever we said as if they were our attendants. One moment they would be servile, and the next they would strike a grand posture and rip apart an important actress's costume. They were completely immoral and seemed like juvenile delinquents to me.

A young man called Ryō-chan was one of them. He was a newcomer to the Peragoro gang, but he was a hard case who stood head and shoulders above the others in his badness. Yet he had not lost his childish innocence, and his manner was bashful. Waiflike, he always wandered from place to place, staying overnight with friends, never going home. Sometimes he slept in his clothes in a corner of the theater. He worked as a legman for a certain newspaper and was nineteen years old.

One day I asked him, "Ryō-chan, why do you hang around here so much?"

At first he was too shy to speak, but then, with downcast eyes and in a delicate, scarcely audible voice, he spoke in broken phrases: "I . . . I don't have a mother." I was moved by his words and felt that I understood him. On that occasion I made a secret resolution in my heart.

I immediately quit acting and began a life with Ryō-chan. I felt I had to watch over this wild youth until he attained maturity. When we started living together, he became completely amenable. Like a gentle pet lamb, he silently fell in line. He was innocent and genuine. I, however, quickly became aware of my own ugliness. Anger, jealousy, and all the other vices that seemed to have lain dormant now began to turn up constantly. I wanted to tell Ryō-chan off and drive him away. I ground my teeth and struggled to control these feelings, but in nine out of ten cases I was defeated. Even when I unexpectedly found myself succeeding in this struggle, my success proved temporary, and soon I reverted to nastiness. I keenly felt that I was the one who needed to be rescued. For me to try to rescue Ryō-chan was a complete impossibility and pure conceit. Carried away with emotion, I had completely overestimated myself. I did not stop and think. Unconsciously, I had decided that I was a correct and pure person. How shameful! Thus I made an abrupt turn. Until now I had sought to help others. Now I sought to help myself.

At that time I lived in Nagoya, then a city full of minds seeking the Way. Every day there was a religious meeting somewhere. "Extinguish the fire! Extinguish the fire! I have to extinguish the fire of bad karma attached to me!"[2] I was lost in a dream. I did my housework in a perfunctory way; indeed, I went out to religious meetings day and night. Ryō-chan never once made a disagreeable face over this.

I attended Christian gatherings. "Good wood comes to a good end. Bad wood is cut down and thrown in the fire of Gehenna. But if you repent and believe in Christ, you will go to the Kingdom of Heaven," they said. "I am that bad wood, no doubt," I thought. However, what I was searching for was not the Kingdom of Heaven. First I wanted to know why I was such bad wood. Neither the Buddhist hell nor the Christian hell was repugnant to me. "May I bravely accept whatever I deserve!" I felt I would not become a Christian.

I was introduced to a young monk of the Lotus School.[3] He had left home to become a monk and wandered about as a mendicant. He burned with inspiration: "In the days of *mappō,* of the degenerate Dharma, we must turn to the True Dharma."[4] His sermons were spontaneous and full of warmth. I became his disciple for a while. "Three thousand worlds are contained in one thought. The ten realms interpenetrate," he taught.[5] I could believe this literally. And I felt that I could settle the problem of the bad wood.[6] "How fine," I thought. However, I felt a certain dissatisfaction with the monk and was unable to fully trust him. He was extremely hot-tempered. When someone criticized him for some trivial personal habit, he would quickly retort, "Those who slander a follower of the Buddha will have their heads smashed into seven pieces."[7] In contrast, the Buddha, who was persistently tormented by Devadatta, says in the Devadatta chapter of the *Lotus Sūtra,* "It was because of the good friendship of Devadatta [that I was able to attain perfect enlightenment]."[8]

7

I Find a Teacher

ONE DAY as I happened to be passing by the Kasuga Shinto Shrine, I saw that there was a lecture series in Shinto beginning that day. I quickly entered and heard at last what I had for so many years longed to hear, a lecture on the Shinto concept of sincerity. There were three lecturers, but the talk given by Rō Sensei,[1] who ascended the rostrum last, moved me most deeply. "Here is my original inspiration! Here is the Way of Sincerity! This is the person I can venerate as my teacher!" I thought.

The next evening, before Ryō-chan returned, I hurriedly left home and boarded a train for Hamamatsu, where Rō Sensei was staying at an inn. I wanted to become this teacher's disciple right then and there and not go back to Ryō-chan. "Oh, if only I can. I want to so much," I thought.

Rō Sensei listened to my request and replied, "Well, I suppose you have the consent of your family, don't you?"

"No."

"That won't do! Quick, go home! Your family will be worried about you!"

I felt like crying. "Well, if I return with their consent, will you let me be your disciple?"

"We'll talk about it then. Do you have the train fare?"

There was nothing else I could do.

It was autumn. In the hedge the purest white bush clovers were blooming luxuriantly.

I turned around and returned to Ryō-chan's. He was a late riser and was still buried under his quilt. When I came in, he opened his eyes a crack and asked in a sleepy voice, "You're home?" before falling into deep sleep again. Seeing this trusting and gracious behavior, my rebelliousness caused me a sharp pain, as if I had bitten myself. Could I abandon this sweet and naive young man? I felt the weight of my responsibility. Until now I had been mother, older sister, and lover to him—could I leave all this behind? If I really could, could Ryō-chan and I really be so fond of each other?

Once my mind got moving, though, it could never turn back. My mind was a jumble of a thousand thoughts, but in the end I could only find peace in the idea of going to Rō Sensei's. One month later I wrote Ryō-chan a letter and, leaving it behind for him, traveled to Rō Sensei's home in Shikoku. I was twenty-eight years old. I had lived with Ryō-chan for two years. "Don't be so careless," I thought.

Rō Sensei's home was humbler than I had expected; even the house was old. But at the shrine, it was fresh and spacious.

"I suppose you have the consent this time?" This was Rō Sensei's first question.

"Yes," I said timidly. I was thinking how terrible it would be if he sent me away again—I had left that letter.

"Well, then, how much time did you get?"

"One year." The consolation I had written to Ryō-chan came unexpectedly to my lips. Naturally, I had no intention of returning.

With the examination concluded, I became a live-in disciple.

Rō Sensei was an authority on Shinto without bias toward any one school or sect. It was well known among his followers that he was versed in the profundities of Shinsendō[2] and was a master of *iaijutsu*.[3] There was an uncanny intensity in his long, narrow eyes. He gave the impression of being rather unapproachable. There were members of his organization and branch *dōjō*[4] all over the country where he was regularly asked to visit. "Could I be trained to become such a great person?" I wondered in admiration and respect. I stood in awe of this person with his unfathomable divine powers.

One week each month there was the practice of Kannagara-no-Michi Shinto in Rō Sensei's home.[5] The procedure was first to sit up straight and still the mind. Then we would purify the breath (with three special ways of breathing) and practice the "heavenly breath." Like the Mu kōan practice in Zen,[6] we sat on our knees with our eyes closed and repeated "oo-oo" with intense concentration. This went on for an hour or more. Finally, we did the "deep chant," taking the vowels *a, i, u, e, o* and energetically singing them out with our whole body and soul, sound by sound, as *u, a, i, e. . . .*[7] Sensei always said, "teaching this discipline is the greatest kindness. The first step in your training is to practice this."

As a live-in disciple, I had duties day and night, and I also made time to pray as much as possible. But I was unable to find satisfaction in just this. Early each morning I went secretly to the Kagami River, doused myself with cold water, and recited prayers in front of the memorial in the park. I felt that if I didn't engage in these somewhat austere practices, there would be no results.

"You think that satori[8] is something that comes to you from outside yourself, but you're wrong. Satori shines out from within you!" said Rō Sensei. I didn't understand what he was saying. In general, I didn't understand what satori was. I thought it was the obtaining of mysterious, esoteric powers. Liberation, I believed, was an entirely different thing.

One year passed. "You'll be leaving sometime tomorrow,

won't you? Are you ready?" I was confused. What was Rō Sensei saying? But I soon remembered that initial interview. "I'm being sent away again!" I thought. What a problem! I had left determined not to return—I felt I had no home to return to. I couldn't face seeing Ryō-chan again. No, I didn't want to go back. Rō Sensei waited a moment as I hesitated and then said sternly, "Anyway, you must go!" There was nothing I could do. I received some travel money from Rō Sensei and with a heavy heart found my way back to Ryō-chan's again.

8

Leaving Ryō-chan

"SO THE KARMIC CONNECTIONS are not yet exhausted, eh? Heh-heh. You still have feelings for Ryō-chan, so it's hard for you to talk freely with him, isn't it? Heh-heh-heh-heh."

The woman from the sweet shop understood well. She lived a rather meager life with her five children, but she maintained a natural dignity and was trustworthy. After my return, I was at a loss what to do and confided my intentions in her.

"So you want to return to this Sensei's place soon, don't you? But it would be better to put it off for now. When the karmic debt is exhausted, things will naturally fall into place as you hope. Yes, unexpected things keep happening, don't they? All things considered, we come into this world to fulfill our karmic debts. Don't try to fight it. If you do, things may go the way you want for a while and you'll feel good. But you will certainly have to repay sometime, and at a higher cost." She was confident of what she said, and her words appealed to me.

I was filled with admiration. "That's right! What you say is really profound!" I unintentionally stared at her face; she had only one eye.

My heart was not pacified, though. Even though what this kindly woman said was true, her words had no power to change my mind. I thought remorsefully, "What a foolish thing I've done! If I take my problems to other people, I'll never make any progress!" I felt strongly that dependency was to be avoided at all costs.

I pondered what to do and searched my heart, but finally all avenues were exhausted. I gave up utterly. At that moment, the name of Kannon Bodhisattva[1] leaped from my mouth. Never before had I ever uttered Kannon's name. "Namu Kannon Bodhisattva![2] Namu Greatly Compassionate Kannon Bodhisattva!" I repeated the forgotten invocation. Suddenly, right before my eyes, about three feet above me, a shining sphere the size of a palm appeared. As I looked, words formed within it, as if written in ink: *You must love!*

I intuitively responded, "Yes, that is how one finds liberation!" I realized that I was always in a hurry to take care of my own problems and completely forgot about Ryō-chan. The reason why I was unable to bring up these matters with Ryō-chan was not that I felt sympathy for him, but because of my own selfishness. If, as before (however blindly), I could truly forget about myself, I wouldn't hesitate now, but would sacrifice my wishes for Ryō-chan's sake. Yet I knew, from frequent and painful experience, that when a strong impulse to do something gushed up in me like a fountain, there was no way I could ignore it.

How was I to go about this "loving," then? It was simply a matter of frankly revealing my inner self to Ryō-chan. Constraint and timidity are impure; they fall short of true love. There aren't two paths in love; if you don't truly love yourself, how can you love another? I felt I had really had my eyes opened. Just as the sweet-shop woman had said, I had been trying to trample underfoot my unfulfilled karma.

I talked at length to Ryō-chan, and he listened to me silently. Finally, in a defiant tone, he began to speak.

"Satomi-san! You think people can be saved by religion? That's a big illusion. What can you save with those lifeless, established religions? They're just playthings for people with time on their hands—just bourgeois propaganda. Can't you resist getting drunk on that stuff? They're always talking about sin, sin, sin. They make me sick, always trying to palm sin off on people. And what about people, eh? I tell you, with a secure income, everybody would be good. There are no intrinsically bad people! And what will give us such a society? Socialism! To save people, you don't need anything else! Socialists are really doing something—they risk their lives for the people's sake and fight for them! They're just like the martyrs of the old days. Really, that's what we should call today's religion. Satomi-san, I place no restrictions on your freedom. But as a matter of principle, I can't let you become a victim of opium poisoning right in front of my eyes!" He was very agitated and wound eloquently on and on.

This eloquence had developed while I was away. And in fact, he was no longer the newspaper legman that he had been just three years ago. Now he was the editor in chief of a newspaper. Of course, it was a second- or third-rate paper, but still . . . . I listened in silence to what he said and thought to myself, "That may be all right for others, but I certainly couldn't be helped by that kind of thing. And I do think I am what he called an intrinsically bad person. But even for a person like me, there absolutely must be a path of liberation somewhere."

At that time we were living in a small single-family house. We were very poor, though, and could barely pay the rent. Ryō-chan used to have his friends over every week and hold meetings of the Socialist Society.[3]

I, for my part, hung a violet curtain in the entryway to make a three-tatami[4] room. There I set up an altar, enshrined some kami, and closed myself in. In that room I said prayers, performed rituals, and so forth. At the end I always energetically chanted "*u, a, o, i, e*" over and over at the top of my voice.

Passers-by would stop in front of the house and the children would imitate me, howling "*u, u,*" as they passed.

In Kannagara-no-Michi Shinto, there is something called Fifty Kōans Established by the Kami.[5] I will give a few examples: (1) Where is the ladder leading up to heaven? (2) What is O-Kami's name and age?[6] (3) What are your four spirits doing right now? (In Shinto they speak of one soul and four spirits. The one soul is "myself before I was born." The four spirits are four basic functions.)[7] (4) Right now, make a cripple stand. I turned kōans like these around in my mind and worked on them with all my might.

I did many other things, too. I tried making up my own interpretations of the Shinto sacred text, *Kojiki.*[8] I visited Shinto shrines. I fasted. I poured cold water over myself in the middle of winter. I made do with only one unlined kimono. I just couldn't resist trying any and every practice I had ever vaguely heard about. Yet even with all this, I wondered if the time would ever come when I would be liberated. Religious practice is a severe thing! At times, I would become miserable, and tears would flow freely down my face.

The neighborhood children often came to play around my place. Dogs came to play, too. The people across the street had a mixed-breed dog named Koro. As it happened, though, they moved back to their old family home, leaving Koro behind. Day after day, Koro continued to sit in front of the house, waiting and grieving for his masters who didn't return. From time to time, he howled in a mournful voice. He would come to me, wagging his tail, to get food, but when he was finished eating, he quickly went back. One day I couldn't find him; no matter how much I called, he didn't come. About three days later, as I was worrying about him one evening, Koro came to me, wagging his tail happily.

"Koro's come back!" Just as I was about to pick him up, I noticed something strange about his haunches. Then I saw: from the throat all the way to the haunches, Koro's skin was split and the two sides joined together again in front, just as Western clothes meet to button up at the chest.

"Koro's been killed!" I awoke in an instant. "Oh, was I asleep? But this is no dream," I thought. "They say if you feed an animal for three days, it won't forget your kindness. And haven't I only just now been feeding him? Just so, even though he really has been killed and has had his hide skinned off, the dead Koro took on his old form and came to me!" I couldn't help crying.

That was a rather strange and gruesome story. Here is another one, but this time it's a story about a person. It happened one evening. A moment after I went to bed, before I fell asleep, something suddenly appeared beside my pillow. I firmly calmed myself until my heart became as still as an ocean without a single tiny wave. I saw the figure clearly. (And I believe that this was neither a hallucination nor an optical illusion.) He was a well-built and handsome middle-aged gentleman, wearing a top-quality kimono set from Ō-Shima. Shortly he began to speak.

"I am Tamatarō's father. When I was alive, I loaned money to someone. This trivial matter weighed on my mind and became a spiritual obstacle to me. After death, I found myself in enormous, weighted leg irons. (They were not put on by anyone, but just became attached by themselves.)[9] I was sunk in a gloomy, narrow place for a long time. But my wife accumulated a great deal of merit power through her habit of reading sūtras before a statue of Buddha morning and night. At the very moment that this merit matured, my shackles snapped in two.[10] How happy I am! I am now in the world of light. I thank her! I am very grateful."

Tamatarō was a child who always came over to play. His mother was an admirable woman who supported four fatherless children by herself. Every month on the death anniversary of her husband, she summoned a monk.[11] She herself read sūtras morning and night. When I told her my story, she listened with an expression of intense emotion on her face.

"That was surely none other than my husband. We didn't know about the matter of the money until he died, when we found the IOU inside his safekeeping box. We still haven't been repaid, and there are no prospects that we ever will be. My husband seems to have had the matter of the money on his mind while on his deathbed.[12] And he was fond of that Ō-Shima kimono set and often wore it." This was her story.

I wrote about this matter in a letter to Rō Sensei. His reply came quickly: "You have my permission to return. By all means come back and practice here again." I felt like my dream was at last becoming a reality. I was overjoyed. "This time everything will be all right," I thought.

From that evening on, a mysterious phantom began to follow me around. It was a thin, short woman. Though she looked young in years, she seemed worn out with family cares. She looked as if she was convalescing from some illness. Her hair hung loosely about her shoulders. She stood imploringly before me with a sorrowful look on her face, pleading for something without saying a word. At all times, and everywhere I looked, there she stood, with the same expression. Only when I stood before the kami altar was this phantom absent.

"Ah! It must be Ryō-chan's mother!" I realized. I casually asked Ryō-chan about her. He replied, "My mother died when I was three, leaving behind four children, the youngest still nursing. Her name was Shigeko and she was twenty-six years old."

"Oh, how painful for her! A young mother—even in the

other world she must be terribly concerned about her children! She must be overcome with worry for Ryō-chan to appear before me like this!" I thought. I could bear it no longer and spoke directly to the ghost: "Mother, please don't worry. I'm going to leave Ryō-chan now and return to Shikoku, but I'll come back again soon to take care of him." I was in earnest; I certainly couldn't try to gloss over a ghost's concerns! As I spoke, the mother's form faded and disappeared, never to appear again.

One more story. This one occurred after I had gone back to Rō Sensei's. One day in the early afternoon as I was doing some sewing, I mused absent-mindedly about Ryō-chan, thinking that parting from a child leaves one feeling sad forever; it's a bad thing. Ryō-chan would always be a child to me. All of a sudden, a peculiar scene was projected before my eyes, like a movie. It looked like some place in the tropics many centuries ago, maybe even in the time of the cave dwellers. A young man with a cloth draped simply around his hips and shoulders was trying to roll a large earthenware vessel (it looked like a water jar) into a mud house. His young skin was tanned brown and he looked very healthy. He rolled the jar into the house, and there inside was a woman watching him intently. "That's me! Ryō-chan and I were brother and sister in a former life! This is how it was then!" I felt I absolutely could not dismiss this as a delusion.

Well, my story has certainly gone off on a tangent. In the end, this kind of phenomenon is a by-product of the practice of religion. The main thread of liberation is an entirely different thing. I, however, mistook the by-product for the real thing.

9

A Fool's Freedom

BEFORE LONG I took leave of Ryō-chan and returned to
Shikoku. Rō Sensei had moved to a magnificent place, quite
unlike his former home. There was an expansive garden with a
pond on the surface of which floated lotus flowers. On the
other side of a thick hedge was a graceful detached building,
suitable for a tea master, in which a high school teacher lodged.
Two businessmen lodged in the main building. Rō Sensei's wife
worked very hard: she prepared meals for the three boarders,
took in washing and sewing, and cared for an adolescent
daughter. There was also a son in the family, but he was
studying away from home. As I write this chapter, I am afraid I
will be criticizing Mrs. Rō. As a disciple of the Buddha, of
course, I must admit that this violates the Buddhist moral code.
But let me begin.

Mrs. Rō was a self-centered woman with a tendency to put
on airs, such as one often sees in middle-class housewives. She
always looked down on others and was never satisfied until she
got a person under her thumb. She understood absolutely
nothing of the Way. Consequently, she wasn't really kind even
to Rō Sensei, while to his disciples she was very cold. One of
the disciples gave her the nickname "Mrs. Socrates." [1] The first
thing Rō Sensei said when he saw me this time was to do the
housework and listen very carefully to what his wife said.

When I was scolded by Mrs. Rō, I used to think, "She sure is

42

hard to get along with." However, since at that time I was more or less Rō Sensei's attendant, her persecution—well, maybe that's an exaggeration—rather, her oppressive behavior was minimized. As I said, this time I had to work as Mrs. Rō's subordinate. The saying about army rules flashed in my mind: "Your commanding officer's orders are not to be questioned! They must be unconditionally obeyed!" I promptly made up my mind: "So! Absolute obedience, eh? Stick to nothing but yes, yes, yes."

"Buy two cakes of tofu."

"Yes."

"No, make it aburage [deep fried tofu]."

"Yes."

"No, tofu."

"Yes."

"Aburage."

"Yes."

"Tofu! . . . Aburage!"

In the end, the order was incoherent, and I didn't know what to do.

"What a lot of trouble you are!" she said.

"Yes," I said, thinking, "I do give myself a lot of trouble."

"Anything will be all right, just buy something!"

"Yes."

"Well, what a fix," I thought, "but I absolutely must obey. Oh dear, what shall it be? What would satisfy her?"

"What? You bought one tofu and one aburage? If it's tofu, make it tofu! If aburage, aburage! Why didn't you make it one or the other? If you jumble them up, it's no good for anything! Why don't you be more careful?"

"Yes!" Indeed, I hadn't thought of that. Well, then? Maybe I am a dunce! Anyway, I don't measure up! I begged her pardon. "I'll be careful from now on, ma'am." (Indeed, I had to respect her. And I really was a fool!) Feeling small, I bowed down to her three times.

From that day on, the grip of Mrs. Rō's ever-pursuing hand loosened at last. I had completed my term and been released. But these mundane episodes between Mrs. Rō and me repeated over and over again, and I had to struggle to keep from laughing. Gradually I came to feel that I really was a fool. I felt free and easy, though. Call it the fool's freedom, if you will, but as the saying goes, "The luggage is all on everyone else's backs, while I, without burden, see the sights of Tokyo." Being a fool was nice, I thought. The always angry Mrs. Rō looked pitiful to me.

One day Mrs. Rō's mother came. Following instructions, I cooked some potatoes and, filling a bowl with the steaming-hot potatoes, carried it respectfully to the grandmother's room. The young daughter, who happened to be there, suddenly grabbed one and, out of the blue, stuffed it into my mouth. I was confused and embarrassed and crept awkwardly from the room, entangled in anger and shame.

When I got back to the kitchen, I broke out in tears. I really regretted my feelings. "What a wretch I am! To get angry at such a thing and lose all my calm, even if only once!" I believed that anger was evil from start to finish and earnestly wished to be completely free of it. I had just been rejoicing that I had finally done it, when this happened. "Shame on you! You've got to get rid of every last shred of this anger!" I shed tears of regret.

How to improve? At first, in imitation of Takitsurudai's wife,[2] I did self-analysis as self-discipline and jotted down my black marks on a little red ball. However, when I examined the ball after a few months, not only was there no progress, but I saw that the black marks had rapidly multiplied. I despaired of that method and tried to think of another I would like. Finally, I

came up with one. The Western masterpiece the *Mona Lisa,*
which hung in the guest room, gave me the idea. That woman
was smiling, always smiling. I gazed steadily at the painting, and
before I knew it, I had melted into her smile. I too was subtly
smiling. "That's it!" I thought. "Smile like the Madonna!
Nothing but a smile! No matter when, no matter where, in the
twinkling of an eye, smile first!" Quickly, before anything could
happen, I cut off all deluded thoughts with my sharp sword of a
smile—and the results were one hundred percent. By smiling
first, I was always clear and bright, and I could handle whatever
came up. Should I meet a ghost—smile; should I fall into
hell— smile. Thus I was always peaceful, all misfortune flew
away, and life was a series of victories. Indeed, there was no
enemy, within or without, that could defeat a smile.

It's been thirty years now since I parted from Mrs. Rō; I am
over sixty years old now. I am healthy in both body and mind.
Whatever comes my way, I ride it out calmly and enjoy the
scenery of the changing seasons. That I can now travel down
the path of gratitude is entirely thanks to the gift of four years
of Mrs. Rō's severe discipline and molding. When I think of her
from time to time, I feel a swelling of gratitude in my heart,
together with such a longing for Mrs. Rō and a fondness for her
daughter that my eyelids soon grow hot. Truly, Mrs. Rō was a
flesh-and-blood Kannon to me, and her daughter was Seishi
Bodhisattva.[3]

> Graciously descending into the six destinies,[4]
> Buddha gives guidance to the errant beings there.
> Each and every being in the six destinies,
> How wonderful! Bodhisattvas all.

Well, I got off on quite another tangent there, but now I'll
pick up the main thread of the narrative again.

10

Shinto Shamaness[1]

NOW I WILL SPEAK of my practices. In truth, I originally had no intention of becoming a *miko*. Ever since I first woke up to sincerity (that time in the field with my father), I couldn't help being aware of my moral ugliness. Tortured with guilt, all I could think of was to somehow wipe away the defilements with which I was stained and to develop the ability to understand myself. Thus I zealously began ascetic practice. At first, I would take a vow and set about my asceticism for set periods of seven, fourteen, or twenty-one days. As might be expected, during the period of ascetic practice, with my body purified, deluded thoughts had no chance to put in an appearance. I felt that, in accordance with my goal, I was becoming completely pure. However, as soon as I fulfilled my vow and took a breather, my true character revealed itself, and in the end I saw that I was no better off than I had been before.

I was discouraged. "While I'm practicing asceticism, there's no problem at all; but as soon as I stop, I'm an ordinary, befouled person. Hmm, they say you shouldn't stop ascetic practice until you lose consciousness and fall into a trance. If I do that, then surely when I revive from the trance, there won't be a bit of defilement left and I'll be an entirely new person." Thus I made the trance itself my goal and took up a final cold-water asceticism. For thirty days in the dead of winter, wanting the water temperature to be as cold as possible, I put water into

46

a basin and left it overnight to freeze. At the crack of dawn the next morning, I broke the ice and poured the water over myself. At night, too, after everyone had gone to sleep, I did the same. I wanted to pass out! I was absolutely fixated on passing out! Nonetheless, I didn't pass out as I wanted. "Try harder! Harder!" I thought. After the morning water asceticism, stark naked, I tried to practice meditation, sitting out on the freezing concrete washstand. But no matter how long I sat out there, I still didn't faint. Then, finally, winter passed. I began to hate myself.

Whether or not as the result of such reckless water discipline, at the beginning of spring I began to experience a great deal of bleeding and had abdominal pains so severe that I couldn't move and could hardly eat. I spent a whole month lying in bed with such terrible pain that I was unable to say a word. I thought I was going to die. But I didn't want to see a doctor. In unbearable pain and feeling that I was at my last extremity, I wanted a chant to cling to for support. "Namu Amaterasu Ōmikami . . . Namu Amaterasu Ōmikami,"[2] I chanted to myself. My mother always used to chant this when she went before the kami altar. Now it leaked faintly and spontaneously from my mouth. Somehow I felt that with this chant on my lips, even if I were to die, I would have no regrets. From this time on, whenever I was in pain, I always chanted this.

I was lucky. This self-invented practice of mine, which I engaged in so strenuously and so uselessly, only exhausted me. I should have been killed, both mentally and physically. With regard to the objective of passing out, though, it was a complete failure. Yet, quite unexpectedly, something marvelous did result from it: communication with the spirit world (i.e., the world of the eighth consciousness) opened up.[3]

Let me speak for a moment about these experiences of the

spirit world. (Please remember that I speak only from my own experience. I imagine there are many people with other views.) How does a *miko* function? For the time being I will tentatively refer to the spirit phenomena that the *miko* experiences as "apparitions of the eighth consciousness." I call them apparitions, but that doesn't mean they are anything weird. Rather, they are perfectly natural things which are manifested when a person passes through a certain spiritual stage. These things can derive either from the human world or from a world beyond. Moreover, it isn't just *miko* who experience the apparitions of the eighth consciousness. All people pass along this way to one degree or another, albeit unconsciously. Everyone experiences apparitions of the eighth consciousness without even noticing. What makes the *miko* different is that she is a specialist in this area, and therefore she is able to consciously pass into this world at any time. Yes, there is fraud, but this is a separate issue.

Anyway, what should one do upon entering this world? One should completely eradicate the seventh consciousness (*manas*, the subconscious, biased thoughts). Once you have done so, the world of the eighth consciousness (*alayavijñāna*, the storehouse consciousness, the mind-root of all things) will naturally appear.[4] How, then, does one get rid of the seventh consciousness? Now, of course, I think zazen is the purest and most direct path. At that time, however, I tried a lot of absurd things.

As I said, as a result of the confused ascetic practice I had engaged in, I had occasionally come to experience the apparitions of the eighth consciousness. And thanks to the "complete idiot" spiritual training I was being given, however unconsciously, by Mrs. Rō, that world was steadily drawing closer. That is, with the power (both latent and manifest) that I had accumulated through ascetic practice, the seventh consciousness had suddenly died—but I hadn't been conscious of what I was doing! Moreover, I had no more than just barely jumped into the world of the eighth consciousness. Now I intended to train with the aim of consciously eradicating the seventh consciousness. This training laid the ground work for subsequently opening up the mind-field of Truth. This was also Rō Sensei's true objective.

> Hit me; kick me; do whatever you want to me.
> I'm a fool; I'll leave it up to you.[5]
>
> Being a fool—an extreme fool—
> I'm sad when the fool gets lost.[6]

When I lose the fool I descend into hell and instantly suffer the pains of the three and four evil births.[7]

> If you're a fool, leaving everything up to everyone else,
> There's nothing in the world you will fear.
>
> On the mountain or in the valley
> The fool, leaving all concerns to others,
> Races up or gallops down.
>
> In the worst of times, the fool, the fortunate one,
> May simply get a good thrashing
> And that's all.
>
> The fool often shoulders the burden of others' wrongs.
> She is forgiven, though,
> Because she is a fool.
>
> People's skin is transparent;
> You can see right through it.
> Mind reading is a fool's specialty.

What? I don't know anything about mind reading! Indeed! Just rattling on and on . . . ah, what a fool, what a fool!

> The beggar and the fool are sages.
> The clever and the student are the deluded.

Misery makes strange bedfellows. Please excuse my foul mouth.

In any case, the fool and the beggar belong to a world beyond the ordinary person's comprehension. The *miko* is the practical application of this fool's world. When a *miko* walks over a path of raging fire, draws red-hot tongs through her hands, pierces her arm with an iron skewer, or walks over a path of sword blades,[8] she is simply doing what a fool does. They say that fools are dangerous and don't understand what they are doing. But the prejudices of the fool's seventh consciousness are dead, so a fool can handle this sort of thing with ease.

I I

Possessed by Spirits

Rō SENSEI was of the Shinto school, but he was definitely not a *miko* manufacturer of the sectarian Shinto type. Again, he was not one who pursued mystery for the sake of mystery, as we see, for example, in Sangaku Buddhism.[1] Nor was he, for all that, a philosopher or ethicist. His true interest was the single principle of Truth, the same as in Buddhism, and awakening people to this Truth. Thus he regarded the *miko* and her powers as nothing but a single page in the book of spiritual training.

Formerly, Rō Sensei had been a Buddhist monk, a disciple of Nantembō Rōshi.[2] Thus his commentary on the "Age of the Kami"[3] in the *Kojiki* was completely in Zen style. Moreover, his *Kannagara-no-Michi Wasan,* which he always had the group members chant, derived from Hakuin Zenji's *Zazen Wasan.*[4] Furthermore, the practice Rō Sensei taught resembled *zazen*[5] and lacked the accretions one sees attached to Shinto practice, like cold-water austerities and the asceticism of Shugendō.[6] However, in contrast to Zen, in which *zazen* is central, for him breathing exercises were the foundation of practice. Both the practice of sitting up straight on one's knees and making the "oo-oo" breath, and the fierce performance of the "deep chant" are clearly functions of the breathing discipline. In speaking of this purification of the breath, Rō Sensei said that one can put both body and mind in good order with one's manner of breathing. He called it "the act of the kami," sweeping all faults and impurities away with the breath and sending them to the far side of the ocean. In positive terms, he said, this practice is an expression of "I am kami; just as kami is in itself, so am I."[7] Rō Sensei said that this practice is completely manifest in the deepest meaning of the Shinto Great Purification.[8]

Rō Sensei published a monthly magazine named *Hi-no-Moto* and occasionally published a pamphlet called *News of the Spirit World*. His "style"[9] was Daigendō Shiyōdōjin, and his name was Maeno Chōji Sensei.

Needless to say, I had gone back to Shikoku in order to be close to Rō Sensei. I wanted to be able to meet with him regularly. But to be honest, though I was pursuing the Way, I really didn't have the vaguest idea of how to go about it. I tried to find the path by taking Rō Sensei's every little word and action as my staff, my standard, and my sole support. However, I was attached to Rō Sensei's wife and had to chase around taking care of all sorts of errands. I rarely even had a chance to be with Rō Sensei and talk. There were meetings for religious practice going on in the house—why wasn't Rō Sensei including me? When I look back on it now, I can see that it was all a gift of Rō Sensei's compassion and I am deeply grateful. But at the time I felt forsaken and miserable. "Rō Sensei sees no potential in me and has lost interest in me. Maybe he intends to abandon me," I thought. I hoped that maybe if I served Rō Sensei's wife, as he asked, I might receive some special secret teaching from Rō Sensei. But as time went by, bad feelings built up in me and I felt more and more dissatisfied. In this way three years passed.

Rō Sensei used to endorse the level of his students' attainment with certifications of beginning, middle, or advanced standing. Even now I don't know what these certifications entailed, but at that time I imagined that Sensei gave the recipients "secret formulas." Among the disciples were two who had received transmission of the middle certification. One of these was a person named Mori-san who, though young, was a master of an advanced level of jūdō. One day Mori-san, accompanied by a friend, came to pay Rō Sensei a visit. As Rō Sensei happened to be out just then, I brought tea to them in the guest room and sat down with them. I looked intently at Mori-san's face and thought I saw there one who was in possession of wonderful mysteries. I longed to get my hands on those mysteries, so I bore in, "What is the deep meaning of the Way?"

Intervening, his friend said, "That? If you're eating, you eat with all your energy and attention." [10] While saying this, he acted like he was shoveling rice into his mouth. Mori-san kept quiet and maintained a passive expression. It was complete gibberish to me. I thought, "These people don't want to let me in on it. Well, that's understandable. It would be terrible to let a word slip and let someone sniff out the secrets you had learned at the risk of your very life."

On another occasion I mentioned to Rō Sensei, "There's a Light and Heavy Jizō I used to go see that's a real marvel. One minute that stone Jizō would be so heavy it couldn't be lifted. Then all of a sudden and for no reason at all, the same Jizō would become light and easy to lift." [11] This was true; I had gone to see this Jizō twice. I really wanted to find the key to this mystery and was very intensely asking Rō Sensei for his teaching.

He carelessly said, "That? It may be strange, but it's nothing important," dismissing it.

At that moment, the words "Heaven and earth are one reality; all things have the same source!" sprang automatically from my lips.

"Yes," said Sensei, settling everything in a single word.

"Hmm. It may be strange, but it's nothing important. . . . You wonder why there should be such a thing as a Light and

Heavy Jizō, but there's nothing to it!" Thus my enthusiasm for the Light and Heavy Jizō quickly cooled. "But," I thought, "marvels do exist! There must be some fantastic, earth-shattering, deep meaning hidden somewhere—maybe inside a roll of brocade, but it must be somewhere! I've got to find it— even just the tiniest shred of it!"

I thought maybe Sensei would transmit the secret to me when I received certification. "Soon he'll be conferring the beginner's certification on me. It's probably a good time now," I guessed randomly. But whenever I brought the matter up, Rō Sensei always stared at me with glaring eyes and kept silent. Helpless, I too sank into silence, laboriously cooking three meals every day. I grew more and more impatient and wondered when this night would end.

Finally, unable to endure it any longer, I made up my mind and frankly confronted Rō Sensei with my questions. "Sensei! I guess I have no potential at all, but . . . Sensei! A tile can never become gold, can it?" I was crying bitterly.

"A tile can't become gold, but if you polish it, it becomes a magnificent jewel." [12]

In my despair, I questioned again. "But even if it becomes a jewel, a tile-jewel is no good for anything."

"That's not so. If a tile becomes a jewel, it's a treasure that belongs to the whole world."

I didn't understand this and took his meaning badly. "All the same, I'm a tile! A tile that will never become gold no matter how much it's polished. You just said, 'A tile can't become gold,' in a roundabout way!" I felt I had cherished unrealistic hopes and wasted my time and effort under Rō Sensei's roof for four years.

As my unhappiness grew, my absolute faith in Rō Sensei began to crumble. Until now, everything he did had met with my unqualified respect and admiration. But now I began to

feel critical and my impetuous spirit urged me to do something rash.

At this juncture a letter from Hokkaido arrived with urgent
news. Father, they wrote, was on the verge of death; the house
had been destroyed in a fire; and a husband had been found for
my elder daughter.[13] I was urged to return home. There were
even travel expenses included as a final entreaty. When I
thought it over, I realized that I'd been wandering around for
sixteen years, wandering in *saṃsāra*.[14] I had gained nothing but
piles of cares and troubles for my parents. How could I face
them, my daughter, the people of my village? I didn't want to
go back. But, things being as they were, I didn't have the
strength to stand my ground. On the one hand, I keenly felt
love and affection for them. And on the other, I was unable to
clearly see a future path for myself. I couldn't bear to just sit
and wait indefinitely. I felt I had to go back.

I made up my mind that it was time for me to return home.
That was when I discovered that I had been severely mistaken
about my accomplishments. The truth was that during my
years with Rō Sensei, the *miko*'s powers were being steadily
cultivated. Thus, before I left I was publicly tested as a *miko*. I
was easily able to walk over fire and blades, and to perform the
other tasks. On the same occasion, Rō Sensei and I together
performed the Pacification of the Soul and Return of the Kami
ceremony, and I was immediately able to produce marvelous
effects. Ah, Rō Sensei! I can't restrain my tears of admiration
and respect! Thank you for caring for me so well!

Let me speak briefly of the Pacification of the Soul and
Return of the Kami ceremony,[15] and of the extraordinary mental state of the medium involved. In the following account, the
guide is Rō Sensei and the medium is me.

Yoshida-san, a fifty-two-year-old grandmother, had asked
Rō Sensei for help. Three years ago she had been seized by a

strange disease. No matter what she'd tried, she hadn't improved, so at last she had sent her granddaughter to stand in for her and receive exorcism from Rō Sensei. So we began.

First, all participants worshiped the kami.

Then the medium sat down with her back to the kami. (It was important to arrange the three abdominal areas[16] in a single straight line.) The guide sat opposite the medium.

Next, the guide offered the Great Purification prayer to the medium three times, conducting himself toward her as if worshiping a kami. (I omit the words of the prayer.) During this time, the medium pressed her hands together in *gasshō*.[17]

The guide next chanted three times the Pacification of the Soul spell. Meanwhile, the medium maintained *gasshō*. Suddenly, something that felt like a lump the size of a fist dropped from the medium's solar plexus all the way down to the lower part of the abdomen—about two inches below the navel and to the left—and settled there firmly. Absolute stillness! There wasn't the tiniest movement; nothing stirred. However, there was a certain world . . . a supremely serene state of mind . . . like a frozen, transparent jewel. Perhaps this is what is called the Crystal Palace.[18]

Next, the guide intoned the Descent of the Spirit spell three times. Abruptly, the medium's hands (in *gasshō*) rose in spirit movement, or rather spirit possession movement. The hands stopped when they reached a level above the head. After a moment, the guide asked, "Who are you?" three times, but the medium's mouth remained clamped shut, immobile. The guide said, "The first time, you can't get your mouth to move," and performed the Open Mouth rite. (I omit this.) A strange rasping sound—clearly not a human voice—flew from my mouth: "Sna-ake, sna-ake, sna-ake," it said in response to the guide's question. And, as follows, it became manifest. I saw it vividly. It said: "When Yoshida-san was twelve, I was a small, one-foot snake. As I lay in the middle of the footpath, the village children returning from school caught me and beat me from head to tail with a stick. They slit my body down the middle the way they do to eels. Six children watched; Yoshida-san was one of them. She was the only girl of the six; she made a face as if she couldn't bear to see my pitiful condition. At the very moment of my agonizing death, in spite of myself, I left my body and jumped onto Yoshida-san's back. . . . About a quarter of a mile south of here there is an empty field. On the east side of the field is a large tree with many branches. At its roots is a small and decaying shrine. You can find me there. Have Yoshida-san put some wildflowers in a sea-green vase and offer them before that shrine. Let me receive her warmth and compassion." Suddenly, a huge snake, twelve inches in diameter, appeared in the upper left corner of my vision and gazed at me with dazzling eyes. "Could this be the former little one-foot snake?" I wondered. "Spirit bodies grow too, I guess." This was the eighth-consciousness apparition on this occasion.

According to what friends tell me, when this was over, I turned around to face the kami and began offering the Great Purification prayer along with the others. As I did, violent spirit movements suddenly shook my whole body. I charged the *kami* altar, hopping like a rabbit. I struck the altar—*unh!*—and became still. The guide had everyone stop praying.

"Anyone who would like to ask something, come right up front and ask," he said.

After a while, someone crept forward and said, "My bicycle was stolen yesterday. Will I get it back?" It was a middle-aged woman's voice.

"What?" I was flustered. The guide sharply yelled, "Hey!" and a bit of dark cloud that had wriggled out of my mind silently vanished. Unconsciously, words thrust up in me from the area of the navel: "The bicycle won't be returned. It was broken down for parts last night."

"Oh no! How awful! That was a valuable bicycle; I used it in my work! I struggled for a long time to buy that bicycle. I had only just managed to get it! . . . Where was the robber from?"

"From the neighborhood."

"I see . . . really . . . and what does he look like?"

"Within a week, someone will be badly hurt in the leg. That's the one." Like a reflex, like an echo, the words flew out. My mind was strained to the point of pain by the sheer not-self. One after another, I answered this kind of simple question from several people. In response, the guide said neither that it was good nor bad, true nor false. As there was nothing further particularly worth talking about, the day's events were quickly brought to a close.

But I was curious. Later, I sometimes got up secretly in the middle of the night and went before the kami. Alone, acting as my own guide, I tried to revive these phenomena. I was always able to revive this day's experience at will and became capable of practicing this freely. In this manner, I wandered from the True Way and fell to the level of a mystery monger, chasing vainly after marvels.

Rō Sensei said, "Even though you're returning to Hokkaido, don't neglect the True Practice I've taught you. You must become the kind of person who can say, 'Thank you,' no matter what hits you. This is all I have to say." These words were Rō Sensei's parting gift to me. Thus I went home abruptly, still feeling inadequate[19] and not wanting my inadequacy to be suspected by my parents or anyone else. If my aged parents knew, they would surely be drained of strength and would lose face before everyone. "What an unworthy child!" I thought. I felt that to proceed was to come to a dead end at a sheer cliff; to retreat was to drown. I was an empty shell, my ambitions, as always, out of step with reality. The demons of unfiliality and misery pursued me, never giving me a moment to catch my breath. "What should I do? Why must I be this way?"

Suddenly a ray of light illumined the gloom of my mind. "Ah, this hardship—how grateful I am for it! This very hardship itself is the favor of the kami. They give it to me because they love me. I mustn't waste this precious gift! Don't they say, 'You must have hardship, even if you have to go out and buy it!'? If it were against the kami's will, I wouldn't be tested like this and I wouldn't be given hope. Without hardship, how could I build up my strength?" I keenly felt the good fortune of having hardship. At the same time, a love for my old hometown boiled up in me such that I was ready to exhaust body and mind for the sake of my village.

12

Return to My Village

THEY SAY THAT my hometown was settled when Hokkaido was first opened up. However, most of the people who moved there never really had any intention of opening up new land as such. As there was a lush and dense virgin forest there, the settlers' intention was to cut in indiscriminately from the forest's edge until the mountain was completely denuded, to sell the lumber and fuel to the cities, and then to dump that place like a pair of worn-out shoes and vanish. Those who lingered behind when others left cried out enviously, "Make a killing! Rake it in!" and in due course they too found something of interest and moved on. In the end, those who settled permanently were the poor with many children and the down and out, those who lived lives of desperation. Consequently, as time passed, not only did the village fail to grow, but it went steadily downhill. Though it was quite out of character for me, I wanted to revive this run-down town.

When I returned to my hometown, I began work as a *miko*. But in no time at all, I was struck by doubt: when I was possessed by a kami and served as the kami's mouthpiece, was what I said true or not? Being a novice, I didn't have the power yet to see into this issue.

At that time, the headquarters of Hokkaido's Ontake Church[1] was in Sapporo. Its president, Yamamoto-san, was the most famous *miko* of the Ontake Church. I used to receive her guidance after I returned home. When I questioned her about my doubt, she answered in a casual manner, "Leave that kind of thing up to the client. Whether you hit the mark or not, whether you are effective or not, that the client will decide." I was feeling dubious. She continued, "Śākyamuni Buddha taught eighty-four thousand doctrines as a device for liberating confused people.' After all, when someone is perplexed and agonizing over a fork in the road, either would do, so to decide on one and clearly point it out is a kindness to that person. 'Did I get it right or not?' is not a serious question. 'If there is any error in what I say, then denounce me, heavenly kami! I know there are those who doubt me.'"

"I see," I said admiringly. As might have been expected, my superior's mind was something special. I bowed my head to her. Still, I didn't have Yamamoto-san's courage. My heart was troubled by uncertainties that I couldn't express.

However, with experience, I was able in time to gain a certain confidence. Let me try to explain my idea briefly. The words which spring unconsciously from my mouth in kami possession, I thought, pour forth from the very center of the *ālaya* consciousness, the unborn, pure nature of mind. They are the real thing. But when, in a flash, the seventh consciousness makes its reflection of them, instantly, the words become shams. This was my idea. I understood it, but I couldn't control its functioning. Yet I thought, "Yamamoto-san is certainly a realized person. The blood of experience flows in her words. In the final analysis, revelations and wise old sayings are born in the *ālaya* consciousness." I was elated with the resolution of my doubt.

At the same time, I was considering the problem of how to revive my hometown. I thought nothing would be better than to create interest in the village by promoting some unique feature of the locale. In the center of the township there is a double cascade waterfall called the Husband-Wife Waterfall. It is formed by one large and one small river, to the east and north of the village, which flow in rapids to a single, semicircular precipice. The water cuts over the edge, raising a mist as it hits the bottomless ravine. One is a thundering male waterfall; the other meanders down the sheer rock face as a sinuous female cascade. Together they form the source of the Ashiribetsu River and thus take the name Ashiribetsu Falls. Again, because Fudō-sama[3] is enshrined there, it's also called Fudō Falls. It is a wonderful sight and is admired throughout all of Hokkaido. Thinking of this and five other large and small waterfalls in the vicinity, I secretly planned to establish a great sacred site in the area.

What luck! A certain ascetic of the Lotus tradition gave me a good idea as to how to go about it. He told me, "Your family has been cursed by the spirit of a dead horse. Because of this, you should go out and get contributions from a thousand people for memorial services for that horse and set up a Horsehead Kannon shrine.[4] Then make the horses of the village pay a shrine visit to it. If you don't do this, sooner or later your family will die out." I didn't know if this was true or false, and I didn't care. But I did think that it was excellent information on how to go about establishing a sacred site.

I stirred up interest in the idea among the members of my family and went out quickly to get approval from the authorities. I worked hard soliciting contributions even from distant towns and villages. Thus in a little less than a year it was done. A Buddhist sculptor had made a stone statue of a seated Kannon, and a modest shrine, about five feet wide on each side, had been built as a cooperative effort by the villagers and other people. The shrine was on the top of Ganseki Hill, facing east, right across the river from my mother's house. On the north face of the hill, several tens of feet of rock wall were planed down. In this were carved four lines from the *Kannon Sūtra:*[5]

> All sentient beings suffer hardship,
> Infinite sorrows weighing on them.
> Kannon's wonderful wisdom power
> Can relieve the suffering of the world.

Thus, though this was nominally more or less my project, I (with my hidden motives) handled matters as broadly as possible, as if this were the business of the entire village.

On the occasion of the Ceremony for the Opening of the Eyes,[6] we advertised widely, hanging posters and so forth. We advertised, of course, in the towns and villages from which we had earlier sought contributions, but also reached out as far as possible to other places. Then, on the appointed day, there were crowds and all kinds of entertainment all day long. It happened so long ago that I've forgotten what year it was, but the day was August 5. Since then, to commemorate that day, a great festival is held every year. There are also monthly festivals in the other months. In addition, I often used to invite a *misogi* [cold-water austerities] leader to come to the site. We would gather Shintoists and youth, camp by the waterfall, and for five days zealously engage in all-night *misogi* training.

There were certainly those villagers, though, who could ridicule me, saying, "You must be possessed by a raccoon dog![7] Thinking up all these things . . . ! Of course, your father's assets are a shambles, too!"

In response I only thought, "I must pour everything into the village! I won't mind if I have to strip the clothes off my back!" At that time father's health was poor and my son-in-law was reserved toward me. Thus, for the most part, I was able to act as my own mind directed.[8]

"What makes life worth living?" I wondered. "Surely it's to exhaust all one's strength for the sake of the world and for the sake of humanity and to sacrifice oneself to this end!" Thus, I gave my projects my all and ran about in all directions. I couldn't find satisfaction in any other way.

And yet, no matter how much I ran busily about, a touch of sadness and dissatisfaction remained deep in my heart. Feeling that my spirit wasn't getting enough nourishment, I began to read everything on moral self-cultivation that I could lay my hands on. Every evening, I took for my daily lesson a text of university lectures so difficult I couldn't possibly understand them by myself. I felt so unsettled by my inability to penetrate even a single page that when I wanted to go to sleep, I couldn't drop off. No matter what I did, all my projects smacked of temporary insanity. I felt their futility—I was doing no more with them than soothing my emotions.

> When you toss a pebble into an empty can,
> All you get is rattle, rattle, rattle.

"I should get completely wrapped up in something," I told myself, "concentrate on it heart and soul, risking life and limb. A diseased and emaciated beggar would be fine. A homeless dog would be fine. A useless old chicken, an insect, the grass, a tree, a square foot of ground, even garbage thrown out without a second thought would be fine. Anything! Is there nothing for which I can sacrifice the last drop of my blood, nothing for which I can exhaust the limits of my sincerity?"

> A lonesome walk.
> Parting the bamboo grass on the back mountain:
> Only rustling and the autumn breeze.

At the same time, without really knowing how it happened, I began to teach about Shinto matters. I lectured as I thought a *miko* should, dabbled in spiritualism,[9] consulted the kami for people, and so forth. I actually acquired a degree of self-confidence in these things and was highly valued as a *miko*. But the empty space in my heart was still not filled. Something unknown deep within my heart kept after me.

"What's the matter with you?" I asked myself. "What is it you want?" I was seriously troubled. "Haven't I found liberation? If I were liberated, wouldn't this cloud of gloom clear up? Why aren't I liberated, despite the mysteries, despite the miracles, despite all my social service activities? I fear I haven't helped anyone," I thought. "Even if I have become an authoritative *miko*, make infallible predictions, and as a one-person social service center save people from suffering and hardship, all that no more than provides a superficial breathing space. Being like this is no true liberation!" I realized that what I had been searching for was not this kind of thing at all. I saw that all the chasing around I had been doing was quite beside the point, an attempt to thread an eyeless needle.

Thus, I promptly resolved to stop being a *miko* and cut myself off from my comrades. I took another look at Buddhism, which I had not been much concerned with until then.

13

A Heart Full of Longing

IN THOSE DAYS, a monk named Tōno-sama was assistant
director of Sapporo's famous temple, Higashi Honganji. He
energetically delivered lectures on the Dharma and also
brought in first-rate scholars and monks one after another to
give lectures: Dawn Lectures, Summer Season Lectures, Con-
tinuing Lectures, Sunday Lectures, Discussion Meetings, et
cetera, et cetera, all year long, almost incessantly. I wanted to
attend as many of these Dharma talks as possible and managed
to leave the mountains for them. Since my pockets were empty,
when I didn't return home to the mountains during the course
of a lecture series, I passed the nights in the Sapporo Jinja
woods or in a corner of the station.

Talks on Amida Buddha's Fundamental Vow[1] always led me
into a state of happy intoxication. However, when I sobered up,
doubts would emerge, so I raised questions at the discussion
meetings in order to have my doubts resolved. After the Sunday
lectures, in a different room, the discussion group sat in a circle
around Tōno-sama. He was both enthusiastic about the
Dharma and affectionate like a father. Because of this, the
discussion meetings were always lively, with an enthusiastic
exchange of questions and answers.

One day at the discussion meeting, I said, "If you believe in
Amida's fundamental vow and leave everything up to Amida-
sama, does that mean that any action committed on that

basis—for example, the karma of deluded people—can be considered a part of Amida's gracious light?"

A youth at Tōno-sama's side interrupted: "That's wrong! From the perspective of our school of absolute Other power, Amida-sama and we are essentially and completely different beings. We humans are deluded beings, thoroughly evil through and through."

I didn't understand and wanted to pursue the matter. "But if we're essentially different beings, then the mutuality of our feelings and Buddha's response will never materialize, will it? Are you saying there's no way for Amida's saving hand to descend? Then where *is* Amida's salvation? What is true peace?" I was defeated, however, by the youth's high-handed manner and couldn't get a word in edgewise. I had to control myself and became silent. In subsequent discussion meetings, this same youth was always serving Tōno-sama and without fail snatched up my questions, obscuring them completely. I was not pleased, but there were also no grounds for offense. I was taking great pains to come and listen, pushing aside obstacles and crossing mountain after mountain, starting out in the early dawn. I wanted at least to return with my uncertainties resolved.

Another incident also occurred during this period. Kandadera Temple's Tomomatsu Entai[2] was to come from Tokyo on a lecture tour. For three days, day and night, he would give lectures and conduct a program, especially for young people. A notice was put out: "Special Candidates May Apply." I immediately called at the information office. A young monk came to the door and, scrutinizing me dubiously, asked, "What is it?"

"I would very much like to join the upcoming Dharma lecture group."

"Huh? What is it?" the young monk asked again, deliberately acting fuzzy-headed.

"I asked if I could please join Tomomatsu Sensei's upcoming Dharma lecture group."

"If it's the Dharma talks, anyone can listen. There's no need to apply specially."

"No, it's not just the Dharma talks. It's also the three-day-long day-and-night program I'd like to join."

In the manner of a simpleton, the young monk said, "Ye-es . . . but grandmother, this group is for young people, so there won't be any people like you."

"I don't mind if I can't be a part of it. But I really would like at least to sit in a corner of the meetings."

"But newspaper reporters will be there and also the director and a lot of other important people!"

Thinking he was saying strange things, I spoke rather strongly, "I don't care. I don't care how many people are there."

Again, the young monk said, "But a photographer is coming to take pictures; there'll even be a radio broadcast made!"

"So what?" I thought. I was displeased and kept silent. The monk kept silent, too. He used his silence to refuse me. I could do nothing but retreat. I was mortified. There were many things I wanted to say. But I examined myself and saw that my appearance was shabby: old, worn-out work shoes, faded work pants, face burnt black by the sun—I exactly fit the image of the old lady from the mountains! Certainly not a person with whom city people could speak freely. The young monk wasn't being unreasonable in refusing me on some pretext. But I was wretched. I cried and cried. I felt as if I would never stop crying.

At that time, Father was old and feeble. All day long he lay on his bed.

Friends said to my face, "You gave your father very much

cause for worry, so in the end he has come to this!" It was just, and I couldn't deny it. I felt regret.

One snowy morning I was alarmed at the dreadful color of Father's face. I instinctively edged up to the side of the bed and kept watch over his stiff, energy-drained features. As I did so, Father suddenly opened his eyes lightly and, gazing at my face, said, "Matsuno?"

"Yes."

"Have the mountain flowers bloomed?"

"Y-yes. With the snowfall that began last night, all over the mountain the snow is clinging beautifully to the three branches, just like flowers."

"No. . . . Has the wild cherry blossomed?"

I was silent.

"Flowers, too, lose track of the season and never blossom, don't they? If squash and cucumbers are late, they won't make fruit. . . . Well, we are what we are."[3]

On hearing my father's heartfelt words, I was carried away with grief. I well understood what he meant. And oh! how I hated my rash and impetuous mind! I would have thrown this burdensome mind into a ditch in a flash! Was there no way I could give my father peace of mind before he died?

> Truth—
> A word seen in a dream.
> Thereafter, the mind
> Is utterly mad.

On the second day of the New Year, in the middle of the night, with snow falling steadily, Father's end finally came.

> When my father drank sake
> He always wept.
> Koshōgatsu.[4]

I was gloomy. Dissatisfied with the Honganji Temple's Dharma talks, I felt I had no religious home. When I saw the perfectly peaceful appearance of my fellow seekers, I felt that I was the only one who hadn't found spiritual liberation.

A memory came to mind of when I was just three or four years old. Late one night, Mother, Father, and I were returning from the theater or somewhere, crossing a lonesome dike. Father was carrying me on his back, and he and Mother were talking happily together as they walked. Being on Father's back, I was gently bathed in his warmth. Suddenly, I was struck by two strange feelings. These were, first, the feeling that I, a child riding on a back, and my parents, talking as they walked, lived in two entirely separate worlds, with no connection what-soever; and, second, the sense that I was a massive stone sunk deep at the bottom of a vast ocean, and my parents were sea foam, floating on the surface of that ocean. These feelings were hidden in a child's heart as bad omens not to be divulged. Just like that, they were my reality, and I felt they were my fate.

As I recalled them, the impressions were quite vivid. Even now I felt like a five-ton stone that could never, never float. But maybe this stone still had some chance in life! I had to search it out! Thus I once again began to rush around madly. Following newspaper notices announcing, "Meeting to Be Held," I ran to religious meetings here and there, fishing among the old, estab-lished religions and the New Religions,[5] taking them as equal. Most of them, though, were rehashed morality or warmed-over mysteries, or again, a drop of this and a dash of that, offered up in a cocktail. In the end, all they said was that their own sect was right.

14

Knocking at the Gates of Zen

THERE IS A Sōtō Zen temple in Sapporo called Chūōji Temple. Its chief priest was a renowned monk, proficient in both learning and virtue; soon he was to become abbot of the Sōtō headquarters temple. Every week at Chūōji, there was a meeting on Zen doctrine with lectures primarily on kōans. I had joined this group some time ago. I felt that the priest's learned talks were truly jewels taken from an infinite store-house. He was far superior to the ordinary religious person. I was deeply impressed by his sermons and admired the personal character that shone through his words. I occupied a seat at Chūōji for a long time, feeling that under this priest's influence, someday even my cloud of delusion would clear up. I heard talks on kōans from the *Mumonkan,* the *Hekigan,* and the *Shōyōroku.*[1] But my mental condition was as usual, and I went around and around in the same old circles. "This won't do!" I thought. Thus, for the first time, I became seriously interested in doing *zazen.*

In the Maruyama district, not far from Sapporo Jinja, there is a Rinzai Zen temple called Zuiryūji. Jōten Roshi, then of Zuiganji Temple in Matsushima, was a former resident at Zuiryūji who, I understand, had restored the temple and painted a picture of Bodhidharma.[2] In his day, they say, there were a considerable number of practicing monks there. Every year at the spring and fall equinoxes, Jōten Rōshi came to Zuiryūji and presided over a week-long *zazen sesshin*. I decided to attend. As I arrived, I saw a large stone signpost inscribed with "Hokkaido Dōjō" standing next to the main temple gate. With the idea that this would be the final and decisive battle, I walked through those gates. It was about the time of the start of World War II.

In the room designated as the *zendō,*[3] about thirty men and women who appeared to be laypersons were sitting in rows before a statue of the Buddha. All of us received the kōan "Mu" from Jōten Rōshi. I felt that at any moment I could realize awakening and silently and earnestly repeated "Mu, Mu" at the bottom of my *hara.*[4] I thought I could surely awaken within the one week. Presently a bell was rung. The participants began to line up in front of the gong and, stiff as I was, I had to go too. So, imitating everyone else, I entered the room. I was completely ignorant of the proper behavior for the room, though. As I bowed to the Rōshi, who was sitting inside, I screwed up all the courage in my body and suddenly, from twelve feet away, let out with, "The Mind is the Way!" This was an intuition I had had once when I was doing *misogi.* I thought that this kind of thing was satori.

"Such a theory is all wrong," replied Rōshi.

"It's not a theory," I thought, though I was unable to reply.

Day after day, in this manner, I rushed on blindly. Then, in the last meditation period, I dimly realized how to fix the direction of my mind. With this boost to my self-confidence, I thought, "Great! I'll certainly realize satori by the next spring equinox! Then I'll be sure to receive Rōshi's endorsement! Satori isn't a very easy thing, though. . . ."

In order to practice meditation, I quickly left my family

("severing all karmic bonds")[5] and moved into a hut attached to the back of that Kannon shrine by the waterfall where, until the previous year, an old charcoal maker had lived. I was accompanied by Chimpe-san, a little dog that the charcoal maker had left behind. Inside, the hut was gloomy. The coarse tatami mats were sooty and laid out loosely, unattached to anything. In a large, built-in hearth in a corner of the room, a jet-black, soot-covered pot hook dangled down. While living in this hut with Chimpe-san, I helped out with the charcoal making and found work in the fields. Living the most meager of lives, I continued with *zazen*.

At first I felt I would reach satori within a week. Then the spring equinox came and went, then the fall equinox, and the spring equinox repeated, until finally the fifth fall equinox approached. I had still not achieved satori! I didn't intend to meet Rōshi personally until I achieved satori; I thought it would be useless. In truth, I thought I would easily attain satori and then meet him. But the more I practiced *zazen,* the less things turned out the way I expected.

"What is this all about?" I asked myself. "It must be because I've got some impurity left in a corner of my heart. The first thing I've got to do is find it and get rid of it." I had probably heard a talk at a temple once about the six perfections.[6] Knowing that one perfection completes the other five perfections, I had made a Hīnayāna-type giving vow.[7] I had tried to fulfill it, but I thought that at some time I must have fallen short and that that failure must be what was blocking my achievement of satori. Something occurred to me.

I had recently visited Mr. K——, who had returned not long ago from Manchuria and lived in the neighborhood. Mr. K—— and his wife were living in a worn-out charcoal kiln that looked like a mud hut. The inside was empty. There were hardly any household goods; of bedding, I could see nothing but two blankets. It was one room without a closet, just like my hut. In this place, and approaching the last month of pregnancy, Mrs. K—— was sleeping, covered with her blanket, when I visited.

"You must be cold."

"No, we've got a Korean stove," she replied.

The three futon quilts I was using popped into my mind then, and I thought of giving one of them to this woman who would soon be a mother. But when I returned to my hut I felt stingy. In spite of myself, I had hesitated up to that moment.

"This is terrible! I've got to knock out this impure nature once and for all!" I thought. So, quickly adding some old clothes to the futon, I returned with them secretly, late at night, to the K——s' place.

"Great! Now I'll realize satori! Surely by this equinox satori will open up and—though a little on the late side—I will have to meet Rōshi!" I was enthusiastic and, rousing my spirits, I repeated "Mu, Mu" doggedly. Thus, at last, the anticipated fall equinox arrived.

But without satori.

And once again the equinox passed.

And yet, still no satori. Thus it became late fall, and even then I couldn't break through.

"Oh, I'm no good! I can't achieve satori no matter what I do! What deep crimes I must have committed! And what a dunce I am! Maybe I could wipe out my crimes with religious practice, but my stupidity . . . no matter what I do, it isn't going to improve! Why should a stupid creature like me expect to attain a wonderful thing like satori?" A flood of emotions forced their way into my heart. Tears fell from my eyes, and I cried out loud. A spray of rain suddenly hit the small window of my hut. The night deepened.

I can't die
With my heart full of longing.
The autumn rain.

I would have liked to die! But I thought thus: "Even if I die, this suffering won't end.[8] Besides, I'm not the only one; somewhere in this world there may be one or two other dull-witted people like me, suffering like me. Well, I'll keep on living! And, along with people I've never met, I'll probably keep on suffering. But I only hope that I am one of those who will awaken to satori at the end of this life. No, I emphatically do not say 'this life.' Even the next life, or the following one, would be fine. And, all right, it's fine even if I am eternally unable to achieve satori! This is my vow! Now that I have made it, it can never in the future be changed!" Thus I vowed firmly in my heart.

In that moment, my tenacious grasping onto satori was suddenly cut off.

As I thought this, I lost consciousness. I don't know how long I remained unconscious, but I awoke suddenly, as if from a dream. In that moment, strange things began to happen. First—and I admit it was hazy—what seemed like a life-soul made of a gaseous substance spontaneously came into being and swelled up and up until it became, in the next moment, some kind of strange and unknown animal-like creature. Like a monkey climbing up a branch, it ascended quickly and agilely. In a moment it reached the top and bumped its head on the sky. Just then, I myself unmistakably became Amenominakanushi-no-Ōkami.[9] This went a step beyond the spheres of kami possession or "oneness of kami and person" which I had hitherto known. In the next moment, the room shrank and the universe was transformed into its essence and appeared at my feet. "Ah! The beginning of the universe—right now! . . . Ah, there is no beginning!"

The next moment, the whole world became a deep blue, glowing and rippling, magnificent whole. "Ah! I gave birth to Buddha and Christ! . . . The unborn, first parent . . . that's me! I gave birth to me! I was what I am before my parents were born!"

These strange, intuitive worlds unfolded instantaneously one after another, as if boldly resolving great issues in huge strokes and with dazzling speed.

"Satori! It's satori! I've awakened! It must be satori!" I snatched Chimpe-san, who was sleeping nearby, up into my arms and walked around the room saying, "Thank you, Chimpe-san! Thank you, Chimpe-san!" I felt as if the whole world had all at once been turned upside down.

> Dew drops, even dust—
> Nothing is unclean.
> The own-nature is pure, the own-nature is pure.[10]

> Kami and Buddha—
> I've searched for you everywhere.
> But you are here, you are here!

15

Sick of Chasing Satori

THE MENTAL WORLD had stagnated in me for a long time without the slightest stirring. Now it sprang abruptly into life. There is absolutely no comparison between so-called ESP, psychic powers, and so forth, and the special mental phenomena that occur when one forgets about the world accessible to the senses. The latter is the vivid activity of the total self.

I spent many days dancing gratefully with the joy of one who has come upon a prolific and eternally inexhaustible spring. Still, I wondered if this was the real thing. I wanted to get explicit certification as soon as possible, but Jōten Rōshi wouldn't be coming until next spring. So I went to see him.

> My unborn parent,
> How dear, how beloved.
> My parent is here!
> My parent is me! Me!

I set out with this and the two *waka* poems[1] in my pocket. Fortunately, I caught the Rōshi at the entrance, just as he was going out.

"I met you five years ago at the fall equinox *zazen* meeting," I said, skipping the formalities.

"Is that so?" the Rōshi replied, carefully scrutinizing my face. "You've become quite an old woman, haven't you?"[2]

"Yes. You've become quite old, too." The Rōshi smiled and

stroked the top of his head. I quickly took the sheet of poems out of my pocket and showed it to him.

After a moment, the Rōshi said, "You've come to quite a good level, but . . ."

"But what haven't I reached yet? And how do I get there?" The Rōshi closed his mouth and said nothing.

"I keep hearing that I must cut off all thoughts and become 'not-self,' but are all the things that come up in the mind evil thoughts that must be severed?" I asked.

"Not necessarily."

"But how can you tell the difference between the good and the evil ones?"

One after another, things I wanted to ask came flooding out. But this was just a standing chat with the Rōshi, whom I had caught on his way out, and I had to restrain my overabundant questioning. I asked a question on the run: "What's the point of so strenuously repeating 'Mu, Mu'?"

"Yes, that's just like putting a heavy stone on top of a pickle barrel."

"I get it! The moment you take off that heavy stone, the passions and delusions pop up from the bottom, yelling 'Nyaah!' just like a jack-in-the-box, eh?" I said half to myself.

With the parting words "Yes, that's right," the Rōshi left hurriedly. He was quite noncommittal. So was my satori all right or not? Afterward, I went twice to pay a call, but both times I was turned away at the door. With things having come to this pass, the vivid mental life of that time gradually faded; the turning wheels slowed. Simultaneously, my happiness and inspiration cooled and finally were completely extinguished.

I became rather sick and tired of working so hard for satori and wondered, "Isn't the suffering inherent in the three poisons[3] and the passions itself each individual's process of religious practice? Aren't the pain and pleasure of the ten

worlds[4]—just as they are—one great state of religious practice? Self-realization or no self-realization, when one considers
that all things are always treading the one path of religious
practice, it's clear that there is nowhere outside this from
which to intervene. It's fine, just as it is! It's precious, just like
this! It's wonderful! Such a thing as the 'salvation of all sentient
beings'[5] is a lot of uncalled-for meddling!" I felt dispirited and
desolate, like still water gradually turning stagnant. "What a
strange place you've fallen to!" I thought. "This can't be the
right track!" But I did not have the means to get myself out of
that place

The following year, in early February, I went to Zuiganji
Temple in Matsushima seeking Jōten Rōshi's guidance, as I
couldn't wait for him to come to Hokkaido. But here, too, it
ended in ambiguity because I couldn't express myself adequately and formulate the right questions.

It was the period before the end of the war when food was
extremely difficult to get. In the waiting room at the station,
below the seat, were the bodies of two people who had starved
to death, stretched out and covered with mats. Starving people,
half dead and half alive, were tottering about on both sides of
the platform, looking as if they would collapse right then and
there. Either they were resigned or their minds were gone,
because their faces had carefree expressions as if nothing were
wrong at all. "Ah! To collapse and die where you fall! How
simple!" I envied those people.

Rōshi did not come to Hokkaido for the March equinox. I
was desolate. Before long, my wonderful experience sank into
the deep shadows of my subconscious.

16

"I Can't Die Before Making You Buddhas!"

EVER SINCE MY DAYS AT HONGANJI, I had been helped in many ways by a woman named Hayakawa-san, whom I called "elder sister." Though she had gone no further than the compulsory education in her studies,[1] her ability in Buddhist thought was powerfully keen and critical. In the course of a single question and answer, she directly penetrated another's mistaken ideas regarding Dharma or self. The average monk couldn't begin to measure up to the power of her insight. Ever since she was a child, she had zealously gone to hear Dharma talks; thus she reached an unshakable conviction in and understanding of Buddhist doctrine. When all is said and done, these were the result of her studies with Shibata Fuguan Sensei. Sensei was a well-known authority on Buddhism and a person of lofty character. Hayakawa-san had been studying the Dharma under him for ten years. She introduced me to him.

Sensei taught us, "Buddhism is a doctrine of no soul. It establishes no objectively existing kami or buddhas. Buddhism's basic premise is that it has no premises. This is its strong point. Also, in the Buddhist scriptures there is science, philosophy, art; you must read respectfully, distinguishing clearly between these. If you don't, you'll become confused and start seeing things in the text like creation by God." I believed what he said. Thus I began to go to Sapporo once a week, staying overnight at Hayakawa-san's house. Together we heard Sensei's lectures and attended the Zen studies meetings at Chūōji.

Sensei was chronically ill with asthma, but he gave his time ungrudgingly to the students who came to see him, speaking to us cordially and at length. Not only that, when one returned, Sensei gave to each individual student a summary of each lecture, which he personally had written out. He told us, "I myself sought the Way, walking a thousand-mile road without rest, seeking a teacher. Since I am familiar with such difficulties, I want the people who come to this place to understand—even if they come only once. I have written this and am giving it to you, so that if you don't understand now, you will understand when you read this later." Sensei lectured each student individually. I listened in when he lectured other students, and this also was highly instructive. I was inspired by Sensei's sincerity and determined wholeheartedly that I must grasp the essence of his lectures.

I finally moved from the charcoal-maker's hut, where I had lived so long, to Toyohira-chō, a town adjacent to Sapporo, taking Chimpe-san along. Hayakawa-san arranged for me to become a maid for a certain family. While I lived there, I had little work to do and received almost no wages, but went instead every day to Sensei's house.

In seven years of Buddhist studies, I had never heard such skillful lectures as Sensei's. Formerly, I had thought that lectures were simply a display of learning and that learning consisted of nothing but labels that were stuck onto things. But I realized how wrong I was. Each word of Sensei's lectures truly became a flesh-and-blood, living thing with real urgency for the listener. When Sensei said, "The autumn leaves: to fall and scatter, fall and scatter is their unchanging Way," I clearly realized that "appearance is reality." As for Hayakawa-san, when Sensei said, "*Ga-te, ga-te:* look! Step by step,"[2] she caught sight of "this moment." Sensei happily said, "She's come to understand quite well! If she studies until next spring, her eyes will open."

Once Sensei said to us, "I can't die before making you buddhas." But the Sensei who said this died suddenly on December 13 of that year, without waiting for the closely approaching spring.

Since meeting Shibata Sensei, I had lived only to hear his lectures. During this time I had gone to school and temple, but this was only in order to delve more deeply into Sensei's teachings. Disenchanted as I was with *zazen,* my interest in Zen had turned toward doctrine. Sensei had taken a true interest in me—an old lady ignored by everyone—and despite his chronic asthma, he had lectured for long hours almost every day for my sake, until the day before he died. My heart was crushed with sorrow.

I determined to finish out my remaining years tending my honored teacher's grave and editing the manuscripts Sensei had entrusted to me of lectures he had given in his lifetime. Sensei's grave was in the grounds of the Higashi Honganji Temple that I mentioned earlier. As for the manuscripts, my part alone filled two mandarin-orange crates, and Hayakawa-san's part filled a medium wicker trunk. In the spring of that year, I threw off my double-layered, half-nun, half-layperson life, which had long been oppressive. I received the nun's precepts from the chief priest at Chūōji. As I was beginning the practice of *takuhatsu* [religious mendicancy], I took up the role of gravekeeper as an appropriate service.

Hayakawa-san, however, didn't go along with this. She dissuaded me from such pointless behavior and lost no time in finding a second teacher, saying that to become deeply versed in the profundities of Buddhism once again was truly to repay the kindness of our honored teacher. In a tearful voice, she said, "Sensei said he couldn't die without making us into buddhas." I too felt like crying.

Here let me give a few reminiscences of Sensei.

When Shibata Sensei was a student, he concentrated on European philosophy. In time he came to a standstill with it, but he was stirred by a courageous spirit, and from then on, with unflagging effort, he hunted in every imaginable kind of publication, visited sages and scholars alike, and finally groped his way to Buddhism. There at last he found the ultimate answer to the great universal and existential questions. Day and night he probed deeply into the Buddhist texts, expounded them for others, and thus became enlightened through his own efforts. He lived over seventy years.

Sensei said, "Buddhism is a religion that has nothing to do with superstition. If you hear the teaching, you will understand it. Over five thousand volumes of scripture simply expound, in various ways, the contents of your own mind. For this reason, even if you don't understand the first time you hear a lecture, on repeated listening you will surely come to understand. Then, no matter what anyone says, an unshakable conviction will grow in you."

As the result of his lengthy and diligent study, he possessed a masterful and comprehensive knowledge. This was evident in his lectures, in which he compared and contrasted all aspects of Buddhism from each and every angle. This was my first systematic study of Buddhist doctrine. When lecturing, Sensei first gave a brief overview, and then moved on to the scripture. He delved minutely into every line and every character, doggedly tracking down the meaning. This may be what is denigrated as "counting black beans," [3] but when I concentrated and listened devotedly, I felt that every word stirred like a living thing, and every sentence tugged at my heartstrings and made my heart leap. Bit by bit, like tissue paper peeling off, I felt I was coming to understand the profound and subtle Dharma. When I realized that, unlike other faiths in which one prays for benefits or miracles, in Buddhism one neither hates hell nor hopes for heaven, but rather lives courageously and eternally in the world of karma, I felt keenly that only here was true liberation to be found.

So I couldn't keep still. While I was still studying with Sensei, I had intended to obtain leave from my employer, rent a room somewhere, and start holding regular monthly meetings to transmit Sensei's precious words. I told Sensei of my plans, and though he had never given public lectures before, he replied, "Well, if you do that, I will go to the meetings and speak there for everyone."

I was delighted and confided my intentions in Hayakawa-san. But for some reason, she looked at me with utter disdain and said, "Boasting already, eh? If you're going to disgrace the Bodhisattva ideal[4] like this, I'm ending our friendship right now! Don't come to my home ever again!"

Now what was this all about, I wondered. Of course, since I had just barely gotten my foot in the door with Buddhist doctrine, this enterprise was a bit premature. But premature wasn't the same thing as boastful! Hadn't Sensei himself given his approval? I was indignant and resentful. But in any case, one cannot take lightly the words of a Dharma friend, so while I was disappointed, I held myself back. When I think about it now, I can see it was a good thing. If it hadn't been for her warning piercing my thick skull, I would certainly have rushed ahead blindly and would no doubt have regretted it later. A close call! Really, the truth of a Dharma friend is a blessing well worth having. While I'm at it, let me relate a word or two about her.

17

Dharma Friend

WHEN IT CAME TO BUDDHISM, Hayakawa-san was a full-fledged general. Her ability to listen to Buddhist talks was phenomenal. On and on she listened, insatiably. As for me, I was a buck private. When I clumsily tried to talk about Buddhism with her, she really howled. One day, feeling that I had a basic understanding of Buddhism, I tried to have a conversation with her:

"When you realize the truth of which Buddhism speaks, you become free of the control of karma," I said.

She, with an air of dismissal, answered, "If you talk like that, you'd better watch out that you don't descend to the level of a wild fox."

"You mean since all things are the product of karma, there's nothing else besides karma, eh?"

"If you talk like that, you'd better watch out that you don't degenerate into a fatalist."[1]

"Everything is an own-nature without own-nature! Everything is no own-nature! No own-nature!"

"What? An own-nature without own-nature? No such thing!"

"I mean, the not-self self . . . it's the not-self!"[2]

"No such thing!"

"But still, you can't help saying it like that, can you?"

"This settling down into 'I can't help it' is not Buddhism."

85

"Well, why not?" I asked again.

"If you don't understand, ask Sensei!" And she turned away.

"Ho-ho!" I thought. "She's a sly one! She doesn't understand it herself, but puts on a knowing face and envelops me in wreaths of smoke with her word games. It's outrageous!"

Finally one day I asked Sensei about it. "Sensei, if I really understood Buddhist thought, I should be able to explain what I know to anyone at all, shouldn't I?"

"Yes."

"So if I can't explain, that means I really don't understand yet?"

"Yes, that's so. However, there are people who understand but don't say anything. Like Hayakawa." I felt as if I had been pierced right through the stomach and knocked flat on my back.

"Your way of listening isn't good enough yet," Sensei continued. "Buddhism is not something you can understand by just listening once or twice. By going back and listening to the same point again and again, it gradually grows on you. Until then, you won't go beyond the condition of one person listening to another give a Dharma talk. You must get to the point where it's like you are listening to yourself give a Dharma talk, or your listening is no good. . . . Do you know the story of the seventeen monks who intended to climb Mount Kyōzan to seek wisdom? They turned back at a hermitage at the foot of the mountain, saying they had already realized satori and that they were busy with the salvation of all sentient beings. What do you think of that story?"

I remained silent.

"Why did those monks not climb Mount Kyōzan as they had planned? Halfway there they felt they were enlightened and thought, 'This will do.' That is precisely what we call sitting down with a halfway satori. They couldn't save themselves, let alone all sentient beings! There is always something more. If you ever sit down with a sense of 'This will do,' you've had it!" My ears hurt.

Hayakawa-san and I met every day at Sensei's house at a prearranged time and heard a lecture together. She had probably heard it all before, but she listened eagerly, saying, "However many times one has heard it, to be taught afresh each time is a wonderful thing." On the way home, she often took me along to a temple or layperson's house where a talk was being given. "Even if it's superstition," she said, "don't think of it as useless, but listen to it with concentration. You will surely find a word or two of truth in it—don't let go of that word!"

This time I bowed my head to her unconditionally. "How true! You are indeed my elder sister!"

In the Toyohira-chō home in which I was then living, I was more of a nanny than a maid. Hayakawa-san's daughter had married into the family there some time ago and now had two elementary-school-aged daughters. I looked after them and helped in the large orchard that the family owned. About a year after I moved there, the family decided to open a restaurant. They gave up the orchard and moved to the center of Sapporo. I went along with them.

The name of the restaurant was Miharu. It was not a first-class place, but though the hostess had just recently been mistress of an orchard, her appearance was elegant and she was a clever and outgoing woman. The waitresses were all carefully chosen. As a result, there were plenty of customers and business prospered immediately. The place was bustling until late at night, ringing with the sound of the record player. Of course, being involved with restauranting, the home was no longer like a normal home. I was practically free all day long: after I had taken the children to school, until the cook came to work, there was nothing in particular for me to do. Just after seven in the evening I became free again and could do what I wanted until morning. The restaurant happened to be within a stone's throw of Chūōji and was also not far from Shibata Sensei's house. Truly, as far as I was concerned, I could not have wished for a better situation. Yet in this occupation there is a certain kind of everyday impurity, and the customers who come to relax, too, are well known for such things. Even though one knows that lies flow freely in this company, one gets caught up in it unconsciously. Seeing all this ebb and flow right before my eyes, I felt that my working in such an atmosphere implicitly supported this evil. I could not bear it and felt I must soon quit. I talked it over with Hayakawa-san.

She abruptly replied, "So, you don't understand that the passions are wisdom, eh?[3] Sensei often speaks of campaigning for the purification of society, but Buddhist purification is not what you think it is."

"Well, what is it, then?"

"In the midst of all the goings-on at the restaurant, offer the waitresses even just a word of Buddhist teaching when you have a chance." At that time, I still didn't know the deeper levels of Hayakawa-san's mind, but something in my heart responded, and I soon gave up the idea of quitting.

Here is how it happened. The director of a prominent Buddhist temple had persuaded a waitress at the restaurant to resign and made her his private secretary. Right after that he sent me a message asking me to come and be cook at the temple. I quickly went over to meet him.

First I asked him, "I have heard of the One Unobstructed Path of Nembutsu, but what is it?"

"It is a matter of passing unhindered through any situation whatsoever, by means of *nembutsu*," he replied.

"So even in the midst of a quagmire, one can pass through unhindered? I see. Let me ask another question. If I entrust everything to the disposition of Amida-sama, shouldn't I leave my present situation to Amida's management?"

"Not so! To leave things to Amida's management in this case is for you to do as I say and come to work here. That is, what I am saying *is* Amida's taking care of things. Suppose a clerk in an office is chosen to become office head. You say that to remain a clerk is Amida's disposition, don't you? But that's wrong. In this case, to bravely quit the clerkship and become head of the office is following Amida's arrangement of things." This sounded like a distortion to me. I felt he had missed the spirit of entrust ment. Thus, in preference to the chairman, a prominent figure in his sect, I felt that old woman Hayakawa-san was the great one. I quickly took my leave of the chairman.

It was the third year of my studies with Shibata Sensei, I think, when Hokkaidō University in Sapporo added Buddhist Studies to the curriculum and approved general auditing. "Will they mind old ladies?" we asked Sensei as we immediately put in our applications. Happily, permission was granted. Twice a week, two hours per session, the lecturer was Hirakawa Sensei, giving lectures under the title "An Overview of Buddhism." His conciseness was the opposite of the minute detail of Shibata Sensei's lectures, and his lectures were easy to understand —he put the point right under one's nose. Even so, I asked Shibata Sensei about things I didn't understand. Thus four years of lectures (including one year on Indian philosophy) came and went. The auditors, who numbered more than forty at the beginning, were only three by the end. During that period there was also a Buddhist Studies program every year in the university summer session. In addition, each of the prominent Buddhist temples had a professional training course. I was spurred on by Hayakawa-san and always attended one of these. Hayakawa-san was truly a passionate seeker. Guiding both herself and others, she was never satisfied until one attained the

Way. First she had taken me to Chūōji, and now again she pointed me in these directions. At times I wanted to flee, but I always succumbed to her energetic shoves.

As a result of Hayakawa's good advice, I had given up the idea of being a gravekeeper and sought a new teacher. As before, I turned to the chief priest of Chūōji as a teacher upon whom I could rely. Thus I privately looked up to him as my second teacher, occasionally speaking with him personally, questioning over and over until I obtained an understanding of unclear points.

One day, in a Zen discussion meeting, an elderly gentleman said, "It's presumptuous for a person to wrestle with the immensity of Buddhism when that person has only a superficial understanding."

I felt that I was being satirized and thought, "That's not right. One is All; if I could just understand one word completely, I would at that moment understand a hundred or a thousand words!"

He went on, "There is no way to measure the unlimited and absolute from the perspective of the limited and relative."

"What is he saying? Who says we are limited and relative?" I retorted in my mind. Aloud, I asked pointedly, "Are you satisfied with that?"

"Being unsatisfied is the human condition."

I thought, "But it's fine being a human being!," and said, "But it's all right being human, isn't it?"

"There's no alternative, is there!" he said.

Hayakawa-san's constant refrain popped into my mind: sinking into resignation like that is not Buddhism! In this manner I came to feel critical of others.

I found myself stuck in a quagmire with one great question, however, unable either to advance or retreat. I heard Buddhism explained as follows: "Buddhism is the teaching of the emptiness of own-nature, of no obstruction, of realizing Buddha in each thought. The Supreme Path has no dead ends; to tread it is to proceed to the ultimate. Empty theory and sophistry have no place in it. Buddhism is the religion practiced by proceeding down the Supreme Path in this very moment. In Buddhism, to move by always moving along is called not moving."[4]

When I heard such an explanation, although I understood it and was able to believe it in a general way, once again something was wrong with me. What now? My feet would not move one inch forward. When I forced them to move, everything seemed hazy and dim. I felt as if I were riding on a horse that was nailed to the ground. I wanted to stamp my feet with frustration. Finally one day, I impulsively approached the chief priest and asked him, "Chief Priest, when I hear talks on Buddhism, I understand each point one by one quite well. Why can't I truly believe it? I have been told that if one understands Buddhism, one will come to believe it. But I can't believe it, or rather, I've come not to believe it!"

A member sitting beside the chief priest said, "That's strange! I, on the other hand, believe it but don't understand!"

And so in the very next Zen meeting lecture I heard, "There are people who 'understand but can't believe in Buddhism.' Such people fundamentally lack the religious temperament!" Thus the chief priest at last drove the spike into me. I really didn't mind this kind of thing, but in this case something was missing: that one precious word which could revive me and spur this nailed-down horse back into life. I searched in all directions, but came up with nothing. I was enveloped in darkness and despair.

At that time, thanks to Hayakawa-san's help, I was sharing the home of a deeply believing gentleman who lived in the watchman's house of a certain orchard. Hayakawa-san's home was next to the same orchard. I went out from there for my practice of *takuhatsu*. Hayakawa-san, though, was strongly opposed to *takuhatsu* and even ridiculed it. This was probably because she was originally a Shinshū Buddhist[5] and regarded lay Buddhism as the ideal.

One day she bombarded me with her usual critical words. "I detest this! You don't work, but rob people of their precious sweat and blood. You have a lot of nerve, exalting your own purity like that! You'd be better off if you'd stop this *takuhatsu* or whatever you call it and turn to the lion dance.[6] You'd earn more! I know someone who does the lion dance—shall I borrow the costume for you?"

I was angry, but I couldn't budge her from her obstinacy. Just one shot of revenge: "Hayakawa-san! If Śākyamuni-sama had performed the lion dance, I would be a lion dancer, or anything else for that matter. But I've never heard of Śākyamuni-sama doing a lion dance, so thanks very much for the idea, but no thanks!"

She kept quiet.

> Please overlook my willfulness, friend.
> Though you blame me for following the wrong path,
> My will cannot bend.
> My life drifts on as a flowing *takuhatsu*.
> If I am ruined for doing this, then all right.
> I can bear the condemnation.

I was so determined to practice *takuhatsu* that I cut myself off from society's expectations.

18

Two Cracks in the Rice Paper

FORTUNATELY, Hayakawa-san and I were able to carry on our unparalleled friendship as usual and without incident. Whenever we met, the first thing we asked each other was, "Have you found a good teacher yet?" As it happened, during my time with Shibata Sensei, I had had a young Dharma friend named Minamikawa-san who once said to me, "Zen is no good as doctrine alone. You've really got to do *sanzen* [personal interview with a Rōshi] or it's all a lie." My friend recommended the Zen Master of Chitose to me at that time, and I remembered him now. When I told Hayakawa-san about him, she became very enthusiastic. Saying she would try visiting him first, she made her preparations quickly and went out alone. She had such self-confidence in Buddhism, she probably had something in mind

To get to Chitose took over two hours by train and streetcar. When she returned, she reported, "That priest is really sharp!" She clearly had been taken down a notch by him. She added, "I made an appointment to visit again at the end of the month— you included." This was May of the year after I lost Shibata Sensei.

The Zen master's name was Suga-sama. At first glance, his

eyes made him seem unapproachable, but all the same, I felt I could open up to him completely. When he met me in the main temple room, the first thing he said was, "I hear you've studied Buddhist thought." I felt embarrassed. He went on, "But that kind of thing is worthless! You don't derive any real capability from it!" I could hold back on that subject no longer, and chattered on and on boldly, even about things I wasn't asked.

"Have you ever done *zazen?*" the Zen master asked.

"Yes, quite some time ago, at Zuiganji under Jōten Rōshi."

"Did the Rōshi say anything to you at that time?"

"Yes, he just said to sit with Mu."

"Were there any experiences that you can think of?"

"Yes." I quickly told him about my experience. That was what I most wanted him to hear.

After a moment he said, "You should by all means go to Mitaka Convent in Tokyo. Please go there and practice for at least a year. I'll give you a letter of introduction." I made up my mind instantly to do so. He added, "Don't forget Jōten Rōshi's kindness."

As we withdrew to the living room, he said, "Because of your experience, there are as many as two cracks in the rice paper.[1] However shallow, satori is satori." I was totally over-joyed. I felt like a jewel that had long been hidden in the depths of a treasure chest had finally been brought out and seen in broad daylight. In fact, I had previously tried to talk about this experience with two monks, but one laughed and would have nothing to do with me, and the other put me off with, "That was just a momentary emotion." Thus I also thought it might be that kind of thing, and since then I had spoken of it to no one.

"Practice in a convent is quite tough, but you're still equal to it. You should go soon, though, before your physical strength declines," said the Zen master.

"Where is the convent?" asked Hayakawa-san from beside me.

"In Tokyo."

"Oh? Chief Priest, her circumstances are such that I don't think she can possibly go off to Tokyo. Please, make her your disciple and look after her yourself."

"The meddling begins again," I thought.

The Zen master said, "I'm busy now; I can't take on any disciples."

"Then please put off her going until next year."

"No!" To me he said, "Go quickly before your enthusiasm cools!"

"I will!" I replied and thought, "There's no need to say anything else! This is clearly my last chance. I'm going, no matter what!"

"You'll be lonely, but you must endure it," the Zen master said to Hayakawa-san.

"Yes, very lonely," said my elder sister despondently.

I returned home and disposed of all my affairs at a single stroke. Going about making my farewell visits, I came at last to my parents' grave. The family had been angry when I told them of my plans, saying, "At your age, going off to Tokyo to practice Buddhism? Grandmother! What's the matter with you?" Their anger was justified. I was unfilial to my parents, undevoted to my children. Yet even I longed for the place where my parents were buried. I loved my family and felt compassion for them. "Oh, why can't my heart find peace like other people's? Will this turmoil never end?" I wondered. As I stood before my parents' grave, bitter tears unexpectedly fell from my eyes.

I had an old friend with psychic powers called the Predicting Sensei. He tried with all his might to stop me, saying, "If you leave here now, you will lose your life in no time at all! Please put off this Tokyo trip for a while!" Two or three difficulties in addition to this arose, but I felt happy about the decision, and my heart was perfectly at peace. I thought to myself, "I still haven't obtained the Way. Time flies like an arrow! One moment is long enough here where there is no teacher; I mustn't linger! Facing my goal and taking this step, even if I were to die now, I would still be satisfied!" My whole body was flush with the joy of this moment of self-affirmation. Thus I set out wholeheartedly for Mitaka Convent. It was the second day of July.

Here are some passages from my journal, dated June 2, 1955, and following:

> I spent a long time reckoning on other treasures—until yesterday I hadn't met a teacher to show me the Way.
>
> An eyeless bird cannot find even its own treasure,[2]
> Much less others' jewels.
>
> I have no time for other treasures,
> Let me concentrate on this one!

June 23:

> Peace of mind: each person's is different.
> If my mind gets out of line, even the smallest bit, I no longer have peace of mind, though maybe someone else could still feel at ease.
> What is my peace of mind? For myself to find myself and become myself.

June 27:

> "To know the time" is to seize the time. To seize the time is just to go along with it.
> They say opportunity knocks only once. What makes it possible for you to grab the opportunity and seize that "only once"? Patience! Whatever you want to say—patience! Whatever you want to do—patience! If you are patient, then Heaven-and-Earth[3] and karma too will offer you a vehicle and

say to you, "Here, please go with this." You can rely on it.

Everybody knows that if you "tune in" to others, you can do anything. To "tune in" ultimately means to become One with Heaven-and-Earth, to function together with Heaven-and-Earth. In Buddhism, this is called 'karma,' that is, being One with Heaven-and-Earth in each and every thought, going step by step together with Heaven-and-Earth. In this way, Heaven-and-Earth, just as it is, becomes one's own.

June 29:

I want to obtain the True Way for myself and for the sake of others. I want to be able to speak of the Way with confidence.

When I arrived at the convent, they were just then in the midst of a *sesshin*. On the door of the gateway was a notice indicating that no personal interviews were being given at that time. I didn't let that stop me, however, and went right on through the gate. As I opened the door at the end of the entryway, I saw the kitchen. There was a dirt floor, a stove, and two spotless iron pots hanging side by side. To the left and right stood narrow, wooden benches. Kitchen utensils were lined up in an orderly fashion on the shelves. In the kitchen stood a very elderly nun. I showed her the letter from Zen master Suga explaining the purpose of my visit.

She spoke softly while offering me tea and refreshments. "Though you have made such a long journey, you cannot see the prioress while the *sesshin* lasts."

"So," I felt, "it seems that whenever I allow myself to hope, I cannot get what I've hoped for. But never mind! Keep trying! With the spearhead of truth I will slash through even an impenetrable barrier!" I made up my mind and pleaded obstinately on this basis and that, but in the end it was to no avail.

"Anyway, you must go back today. Later, when the prioress is available, you can come back and meet her. Suga-san himself once had to make these advance inquiries, so please . . . ," the nun said, at something of a loss. I thought to myself, "If I take this kind of long-drawn-out approach, anything might happen! Chipping away bit by bit, I'll never get anywhere! This is desperate—I've got to do something!" I had no place to go, but nevertheless I was being dismissed.

"Do you know anyone around here?" asked the nun.

"Yes, but I don't know the address. The name is Mina-mikawa."

"Oh, from Hokkaido. Yes, Minamikawa-san has been here. Wait a minute, please." So saying, the nun went off in the direction of the main hall and returned momentarily.

"Minamikawa-san was formerly at Taiheiji, so you can find the information there." Handing me a piece of paper with the directions, she added, "The Rōshi there is a sincere and ardent practitioner."

A young nun not only accompanied me to the streetcar stop, but also took the streetcar with me and saw me to the station near Taiheiji. This thoroughgoing kindness touched me deeply; I thus indirectly felt the warmth of the prioress's kind and exalted spirit.

On the way to Taiheiji, I spoke freely with the young nun. "I've heard that a monk or nun gets *kenshō* but that a layperson can only hear about enlightenment secondhand," I said. "Is it so?"

"Oh? I have never heard such a thing said.[4] Who says so?"

"A monk."

"Oh? Well, I don't think that's so."

"I agree." I was happy that she agreed with me.

I got Minamikawa-san's address at Taiheiji, but unfortunately, when I went there my friend was out and was not expected to return for two or three days. There was nothing else to do but retreat to Taiheiji. I don't mind sleeping outside, but I was tired. Tonight at least I wanted to sleep with a roof over my head. So I revealed my situation to the Rōshi's wife and shamelessly asked for a night's lodging.

19

Knocking Over Flagpoles

PLEASE, DO STAY HERE. The Rōshi should be back soon,"
the Rōshi's wife consented cheerfully.

"Thank goodness! Thank you so much!" I thought.

When the Rōshi returned, he showed me to the public bath,
where I relaxed and unwound. When I left the bath, the Rōshi
was waiting for me at the entrance. I was very grateful. "What
a kind person!" I thought.

I expected to take my leave early the next morning, but
Rōshi asked, "Why not stay here until things are settled at the
convent?" I was happy to hear him say that, but I couldn't help
thinking it over. There was no reason to believe I would ever be
able to repay this kindness, even partially, and that troubled
me. I hesitated for some time, but in the end I accepted the
offer.

Four days later word came from the convent, and I quickly
went there.

The prioress was gentle and kind, yet she also possessed
great mental power, unmarred by the tiniest flaw. Once the
greetings were dispensed with, she said, "I have thought a great
deal about you. . . . I think it would be best if you were to live
in a believing layperson's home and travel from there back and
forth to the convent for religious training. I'm looking for such
a home for you now."

"Oh no!" I thought. "That's terrible! That might be all right for somebody else, but for me it's no good. I've got to be admitted!" I well understood that the prioress was concerned about me. But really, the dilemma of my double life had given me no end of trouble for many years. I had finally come to feel that I absolutely had to stop straddling the fence—I must be either laywoman or nun. If I couldn't practice Buddhism in the convent, so be it! But to practice like that, going back and forth, would be no practice at all!

I concentrated my resolve. "Don't underestimate the power of sincerity!" I thought. "As long as I have breath, even if 'like dew at the edge of a field, I vanish,' I will push straight ahead, despite mountains, despite rivers! If I fall down, I'll get up again! If I stumble, I'll right myself! Just advance! Just advance! To either life or death!"

"I want to practice *takuhatsu,* but it's not right to do so as a laywoman," I said as I had planned.

"Do you have any relative hereabouts, or someone who could guarantee you?"

"No." I guarantee myself! But I suppose that insofar as I am my own guarantee, there is no assurance.

"If you became ill, it would be a problem, wouldn't it?"

"Please don't concern yourself over that!" I thought there was no need to worry about such things before they happened.

"You shouldn't say that. In such a case, you become a problem to those around you."

"Yes, you're right. . . ." I gave in.

After we had gone back and forth with several questions and answers, the prioress said, "We have an age limit at this convent; only women in their twenties or thirties may enter."

"Aha, the trump card! Did I fail the test? Well, I guess there's no point in further discussion," I thought. Nonetheless, I kept trying. I asked her, "Can't something be done about that?"

"No. We can't break the rules of the convent just for you."

"Of course. So here, too, I am defeated," I thought. I tried one last approach. "If you cannot consent to have me as a practitioner, can't you find some kind of use for me? Anything at all, I won't mind! I'll do anything, anything! But please just let me stay in some corner. I beg you!" Unexpectedly, a teardrop rolled off my face. I bowed down. There was nothing more to say. My ammunition was exhausted.

In the end, the convent doors would not open for me. Once again I had exhausted the bottommost depths of my heart. I had tried my best. There was nothing to be done about it! There was no karmic tie. Thus I was satisfied and felt no regrets.

I returned to Taiheiji to tell the Rōshi of the poor outcome at the convent. "Well, what will you do?" he asked.

"Go back to Hokkaido, I suppose." I was thinking of going to see Zen master Suga.

"But you went to so much trouble to come here from Hokkaido to practice Buddhism."

"Yes," I said, feeling a sudden tightness in my chest.

Rōshi said, "Maybe you could stay here. . . ." After a pause he added, "Well, think it over carefully." I was pierced to the marrow by this compassion. However, since this was something I couldn't very well decide with my heart, I postponed the reply until the next morning. I had two problems. First, I considered, I would feel bad if I couldn't give Zen master Suga an account of the whole course of events. And second, I wondered if I could really presume upon the kindness of the Rōshi and his wife like this. But, I thought, besides practicing Zen, I could help out the wife for a month or two and then return home. Thus I stayed on.

The Rōshi took me to the Zen meetings at Sōseiji Temple in Nakano. There for the first time I heard *teishō*.[1] It was brusque and plain yet had a wonderful power. I listened with intense concentration, holding my breath. But in fact, I didn't understand well. Again, the Rōshi spoke to me in detail about *zazen*—the right way to do it, things to watch for, and so forth. This too was something I was happy to hear at last. I was deeply impressed by this meticulous guidance, which exhausted the limits of kindness. Finally, I made up my mind to engage in really thorough practice with Rōshi.

Though I didn't neglect my other duties for my own individual practice, I felt I must first and foremost sit in *zazen*. Thus I rose early every morning and meditated, facing a wall in the corner of the kitchen. While doing *zazen*, various important but previously overlooked questions frequently came to mind. At such times I always asked Rōshi about them and received an explanation. In other cases too, whenever problems arose, I always received guidance. I tried never to let questions linger in my mind. Thus, after a month in Tokyo, I received permission to join a five-day *sesshin* at Shinkōji Temple.

At the first *dokusan*,[2] Rōshi examined my mental state. Even there I couldn't help speaking of the baggage of past experiences that I lugged around.

Rōshi said, "That is *makyō*.[3] Please try to start all over again."

"Really?" I thought. "All right, if that's the case, I *will* get a fresh start." Thus making up my mind, I sat enthusiastically with Mu. But all of a sudden—were the old experiences of sinking into kami possession working their mischief?—I slipped into a state of blankness, as though drunk. When I came to my senses, I thought, "This is no good!" and tried to have another go at it. But no matter how many times I started over, each time I was captivated before I knew it and drawn into the lair. Thus the *sesshin* came to an end in this indefinite state.

Again, Rōshi took me to the Zen meetings at Tokorozawa's Raikōji Temple. There, once a month, there was *zazen* and *teishō*. This time the *teishō* was on the *Mumonkan*'s "Kashō and the Flagpole."[4] The tatami mats of the main hall at Raikōji were worn at the edges and tattered. When I saw that, I found myself thinking, "When I worked as a *miko,* business really thrived; I could have easily had these mats fixed. Maybe I should become a *miko* again! Even that isn't altogether useless in the work of liberating the dead who have lost their way."

Just then—"Aha!"—I caught myself. "You fool! That's the flagpole! Yes—when the merest glance casts a reflection in your mind, that's the flagpole! Knock over that flagpole in your mind! One after another, knock them down!" This is how I took "Kashō and the Flagpole." Until now my *zazen* practice had been grasping at clouds. Now I had discovered a principle to guide my practice. I thought to myself that I must never lessen the tension in my *hara.*[5]

20

Joy

THERE WAS NO August *sesshin* at Shinkōji Temple, so I'll go on to the September *sesshin*.

It was the second day of the *sesshin*. I was working very hard with my *hara,* saying, "Mu, Mu," when all of a sudden—"Unh!"—it was as if three people had pulled me over backward. "Oh no!" I thought. I repulsed this with effort, straightened my posture, and resumed, "Mu, Mu." Then again "Unh!"—I was dragged down.

"This is awful!" I thought. I kept trying to pull myself together, but no matter how many times I tried, it was no use. "What now?" I thought. "I wonder if I'm dozing off." When the walking meditation[1] was over, I thought to myself, "Okay, now!" and sat, hardening my *hara* all the more. As I did so, once again it started. "Very strange," I thought. "I know! It's a possessing spirit! The spirit of a dead person." (In possession by spirits of the dead, one is thrown onto one's back, facing up; in the case of spirits of the living, one is pushed over onto one's face.) "I don't know if it's a good spirit or a bad spirit, but there's more than one of them, anyway! . . . Okay. . . ."

"Hey! Everybody!" I said silently to the spirits. "Wait a minute, please! When I attain *kenshō,* I will without fail perform a memorial service for you. Until then, please be patient and wait quietly on the spirit shelf."[2] With this statement to free me of their presence, I sat with all the more intense effort.

After that, I was not dragged over as badly as before, but if my effort slackened even a little, I was instantly pulled down. This continued all day.

I was dead tired. That evening when I tried to settle down to sleep, the instant I laid my head on the pillow, I saw: "Ah! This out-breath is Mu!" Then: "The in-breath too is Mu!" Next breath, too: Mu! Next breath: Mu, Mu! "Mu, a whole sequence of Mu! Croak, croak; meow, meow—these too are Mu! The bedding, the wall, the column, the sliding door—these too are Mu! This, that and everything is Mu! Ha ha! Ha ha ha ha ha! That Rōshi is a rascal! He's always tricking people with his 'Mu, Mu, Mu'! . . . Hmm. I wonder if, after this, I should rush to Rōshi's room for *dokusan*. No, that would be childish. . . ."

I felt as if a chronic disease of forty years had been cured in an instant. I slept soundly that night.

Very early the next morning was *dokusan*. Abruptly, I said, "Rōshi, I saw Mu." At least I was able to say that much clearly. Then Rōshi examined me in a number of ways, and *kenshō* was confirmed.

"You slept soundly last night, eh?" asked Rōshi.

"Yes, I slept well," I answered truthfully. They say that the night after *kenshō*, you can't sleep for joy, but that wasn't the case for me; my mood wasn't particularly affected. "For some reason, I feel quite calm," I thought. I felt as if I had finally gulped down some big thing that had been stuck in my throat a long time. And the fog in my mind had all at once lifted. I thought, "So this is *kenshō*, eh? If even a dull person like me is able to see Mu—albeit ever so slightly—then in the whole world there isn't a single person who can't attain *kenshō*! 'Seek and you will find. Look and you will see. Knock and it will be opened to you.'[3] That's right! That's true!"

"Visiting Zenkōji Temple, drawn by an ox."[4] I had been drawn by a mind which sought. It seemed as if I had been going around and around in circles, repeating the same mistakes over and over for forty years. But now that I have awakened from the dream and can see clearly, I know that the saying "You don't have the same experience twice" is really true. Not a single step is given to repeating the past or to useless efforts. I can see now that things which seemed redundant or insignificant at the time were all necessary conditions for what followed.

It is also clear to me that the return of this lost child to the original home for which she has longed is a gift. I have returned home thanks to the compassion and skill of the buddhas and bodhisattvas. "Amida's five aeons of practice was for me, Shinran, alone."[5] Ah, thank you! Thank you! All things in the universe have together nurtured small and insignificant me. They have given their very lifeblood for my sake.

> Ah, hardship—more and more it accumulates.
> I have my limits, but I will try with all my might.
> Pressure makes you into a jewel.

These verses have been with me constantly since beginning Buddhist practice. They always spur me on and arouse feelings of aspiration and gratitude. They are the words of an enlightened person—my beloved teacher. Today, let me return them to him[6] to express my gratitude for his kindness:

> To exist is to accumulate hardship.
> Only thus can my life continue to flow.
> *Gasshō*

And so we come to the next month when, on the twenty-seventh of October, I renewed my nun's vows with Rōshi and received the tonsure (until then I had kept my hair). On the same occasion I received the Buddhist name Daien Myōdō from the chief priest at Chūōji. And thus I have continued to the present. How strange and wonderful is the world of karma.

It may be superfluous, but I would like to add another comment. It is difficult to meet a true teacher. Without a true teacher, one cannot obtain the True Way. If perchance one were to find it, one could not master it. Now, this is really presumptuous, but let me say one more thing. When I think of certain famous persons over whom everyone makes a fuss, such as the founders of certain religions,[7] I am appalled. When, in their practice of austerities, some abnormal phenomena arise in body or mind, they get carried away. They settle down in this condition and get the idea into their heads that "This is the Supreme Way of Heaven-and-Earth!" There are even cases of people who affect, "In all the universe, I alone am to be revered!"[8] Isn't it really a matter of regret and chagrin that a human being can claim to be the spiritual leader of all existence? Even so, to meet an open-eyed teacher is a momentous thing.

Let me quote a passage on "Gratitude-Based Practice" from Yasutani Rōshi's "Song in Praise of Practice-Realization." He writes, "Even if someone has a harmonious personality, a pure character, and high morality, has studied Buddhism deeply, is broad-minded, speaks eloquently, is an excellent calligrapher, writes wonderful prose and poetry, and even has profound *samādhi* power,[9] if that person does not pass the empty-mind test,[10] karma is still produced. Though a highly respected friend, such a person is of no use whatsoever for the Way of Liberation." I experienced this keenly. There isn't a shadow of a doubt about it. Fortunately, thanks to Rōshi, I found my mind's serenity at last.

I, who had made a 180-degree turn once before, turned another 180 degrees. Truly, I turned 360 degrees and arrived at the original starting point:

Arriving, I look about.
There are the flowers of my old home.
Instead of myself there is the *mani* jewel,[11]
Grasped firmly in this hand.

Ah! I am the happiest person in the world! I'm a billionaire! Besides this, what more could I want? Now all that remains is to show my mind to you, my teacher, and receive your guidance.

My teacher's goodness is deeper than the bottomless ocean.
How could I ever repay it?

Since *kenshō,* I have been working with kōans, one after another. Every time I penetrate a kōan, a thin skin peels off my mind. Layer by layer, the mind's foundation is gradually becoming clear. Thus the more I enter into the ocean of Buddha Dharma, the more I understand how deep it is. And yet its content is nothing at all.[12] A human life filled with this "nothing at all" is a marvelous thing.

When I think nowadays of my deceased father and mother, I am filled with deep emotion.

Much time has already passed
Since the grasshoppers have been watching from the shadows of the
     grass.[13]
In the next life, I'll be the child of the same parents again.
I'll be a good child, to my heart's content.

I've written at great length. I'm embarrassed that it may seem like self-advertisement.

Awakening from the dream, I see:
Sincerity is simply my original nature.
Where, then, shall I look for it?

Epilogue

FOLLOWING HER KENSHŌ EXPERIENCE, Satomi-san continued for years in her study of Zen with Yasutani Rōshi. She successfully passed each kōan in the entire kōan series, thus completing her formal Zen training. Even with the kōans behind her, she continued the practice of Zen for the rest of her life; enlightenment, it is said, can be deepened infinitely. The completion of the kōan series, however, put her in a position in which, with her teacher's permission, she might have proceeded to become a Zen teacher. Ironically, though she had many times prematurely (as she later saw it) set herself up as a spiritual teacher, now that she really was in a position to authentically take on such a role, she chose not to do so. Instead, she preferred to encourage people to study with Yasutani Rōshi.

Most of the rest of her life was spent as an assistant to Yasutani Rōshi. For many years she attended to the nonteaching chores that kept Taiheiji running: cooking, leading the chanting, drawing well water and heating it for the bath, and so on. When the Rōshi traveled, she and one or two other senior disciples accompanied him. She was content. She had found what she had spent a lifetime looking for.

Finally, when she was almost eighty years old, Satomi-san returned home to Hokkaido for the last time. Though she had grown somewhat forgetful, she was healthy and continued her Zen practice. She entered a nursing home and died there on

August 2, 1978, at the age of eighty-two. She was buried in the family grave in the village graveyard. Her friends remember her as a veritable Kannon: always calm, quiet and self-effacing, with a broad, beaming smile and infectious laughter.

Notes for Part One

1. MORAL EDUCATION

1. Karma is the Buddhist law of cause and effect. According to this concept, everything that happens in the present is the result of past actions, whether committed in the present life or in a previous life. What Satomi-san means here is that her good fortune in finding instruction and a teacher at Taiheiji Temple was not a matter of chance or luck, but the inevitable result of things she had done in the past. Furthermore, the people at Taiheiji Temple had also done things in the past which determined that they would someday help Satomi-san. Of course, Satomi-san did not know she would go to Taiheiji, and the people at Taiheiji did not know she would come. But the karmic link or connection between them existed before their meeting and determined that that meeting would occur.

2. An intensive meditation retreat in which the participants withdraw temporarily from contact with nonparticipants.

3. This parable is found in the *Lotus Sūtra,* chapter 4, "Belief and Understanding." The story is as follows: A boy runs away from home. His father is distraught and searches for him, but in vain. More than fifty years pass while the son wanders in distant places, growing ever poorer. Meanwhile, his father moves to a new city and becomes extremely rich. He longs for his son, as he is growing old and has no other heir, but he speaks of his longing to no one. One day the son happens to wander into the city where his father has settled. He sees his father surrounded by riches and, instead of recognizing him, mistakes him for a great king or other royal person. He turns to leave. His father, who has seen and recognized him, sends his attendants to bring his son to him, without explaining the son's identity to them. The son, thinking he is being arrested, becomes terrified and faints. On seeing this, the father tells the attendants to release him, and the son leaves for a nearby village. In order to bring his son back, the rich man realizes

that he must overcome his son's fear gradually. So he sends men to ask the son to come work for him as a dirt laborer for good wages. The son comes and works. As twenty years pass, the father gradually raises his son's position, giving him higher wages, a servant, and more responsibility, and telling him he wants to treat him as his son. Finally, feeling that he will die before long, the rich man reveals to one and all that this man is truly his son and heir. Thus the story ends. The text explains that the rich man is the Buddha and each of us is the son. We all will finally wander back to our original home and·with the help of Buddha discover the riches of enlightenment, which were ours all along, though we were ignorant of them. Cf. Leon Hurvitz, trans., *Scripture of the Lotus Blossom of the Fine Dharma* (New York: Columbia, 1976), pp. 84–100.

4. Satomi-san apparently entered Girls' High School about 1908. At this time, elementary schools were coeducational, but education was sex-segregated thereafter and girls went straight from elementary school to Girls' High School. In 1900, four years of education were universally compulsory; in 1907, this requirement was raised to six years. Few girls received an education beyond elementary school in this era in Japan. For a poor country girl like Satomi-san to go on for further education was remarkable indeed, especially considering that she was an only child and her labor was needed at home. Moreover, the school she attended was an elite institution. Satomi-san was clearly both very bright and very much indulged by her parents. As for the school motto, this was the staɴdard motto for female education at the time.

5. Filial piety is a fundamental virtue in Japan. It involves not only respecting and obeying one's parents, but caring for their needs and serving them as well. Ideally, one should forget oneself and act to fulfill one's parents' wishes.

2. SINCERITY

1. Satomi-san, in line with her culture, equates a fatherless child with an orphan.

2. Satomi-san means that her state of mind had been "normal" until the time her husband left. Buddhists, however, see this apparently normal state as a deeply deluded condition. This reference to the sixth consciousness, or *manovijñāna* in Sanskrit, introduces us to a complex exposition on the nature of the mind and its functions according to

Buddhist psychology. This system will be discussed in more detail later in the text. For now, suffice it to say that the sixth consciousness is the principle of delusion, i.e., that aspect of the mind which discriminates between "me" and "not me" and hence gives rise to egotism, selfish desires, and self-centered behavior.

3. MY STRANGE MENTAL CONDITION

1. This is Satomi-san's given name until she takes on the Buddhist name Myōdō.
2. In other words, the roots of evil have been severed already in the spirit world, so Satomi-san is commanded simply to take care of the leaves and branches of evil—an easy job with the roots already cut
3. Kami are spirits or deities that are traditionally believed to inhabit Japan. Mountains, islands, stones, fields, the sky—kami may be found anywhere the Japanese feel the presence of the numinous. Shrines to the kami are found throughout Japan.
4. This was written in 1956, so of course the thirty yen of that day would be worth a great deal more now.

4. I LOSE MY BABY

1. Koishikawa is a neighborhood in Tokyo.
2. Fermented soybeans, a popular breakfast dish.
3. Kanda is a neighborhood in Tokyo.
4. According to a popular Japanese legend, Sai-no-Kawara is a dry river bed at the entrance to the world of the dead where children go when they die. There they gather stones to try to build towers for memorial services for their parents, in an effort to fulfill their filial obligations. No matter how many times they build the towers, though, demons always come along and smash them to bits. The Buddhist savior Jizō Bodhisattva is said to rescue the children from this suffering.

5. COMPLETE NERVOUS BREAKDOWN

1. Fujimura Misao (1886–1903) was a student at an elite high school. He committed suicide by throwing himself into the Kegon Waterfall at Nikkō, leaving behind a suicide note in which he asserted, "Life is incomprehensible." This suicide occurred at a time of rapid social and

cultural change in Japan and was taken as indicative of the times, a symptom of the tremendous demands being made on the Japanese people. The suicide was a great shock to the people of the Meiji era.

2. The coat and nightgown are kimono-style.

3. This poem is quoted from the famous haiku poet Bashō. According to T. P. Kasulis, Bashō expresses in this haiku "the Zen qualms about putting things into words." Satomi-san's use seems to be less epistemological and more emotional. I take her meaning to be: "Whatever I say, it isn't right; I should keep silent." Cf. T. P. Kasulis, *Zen Action Zen Person* (Honolulu: University Press of Hawaii, 1981), p. 28.

4. *Kageki* is a kind of theater, much like an operetta or a musical revue. The plays have simple plots and depend heavily on music and staging for their popular appeal. The cast is all female, the actresses playing both male and female roles. It was most popular in the Taishō era (1912–1926) but can still be seen today.

6. KAGEKI ACTRESS

1. *Peragoro* means "opera bums." During the Taishō period, these gangs were quite commonly found attached to the *kageki* troupes, following the actresses around, wandering freely in and out of the theaters, and generally making a nuisance of themselves.

2. In Buddhism, fire is a symbol for the passions, the emotions conditioned by ignorance. Fire also symbolizes the idea that the ordinary human condition is, in fact, a state of emergency calling for immediate and drastic response (namely, Buddhist practice).

3. That is, the Nichiren school, founded by Nichiren (1222–1282) in 1253. The school takes the *Lotus Sūtra* as its foundation.

4. According to the Nichiren school (and some other Buddhist schools), the Buddha had predicted a steady decline in humanity's ability to preserve, understand, and practice the Buddha's teachings, i.e., the Dharma. *Mappō* was the final period of greatest degeneracy in which people would no longer be able to practice Buddhism properly. Nichiren taught that his age was the age of *mappō*. The True Dharma for the degenerate *mappō* period, according to Nichiren, is to turn one's back on traditional Buddhist practices such as meditation and focus exclusively on the veneration and study of the *Lotus Sūtra*. The central practice of the school is the repetition of "*Namu Myōhō Rengekyō*" ("Praise to the *Lotus Sūtra*"). This "simple" practice was held to be an

appropriate replacement for the former "difficult" practices, since humanity was thought to be no longer capable of the latter.

5. The first sentence of the quotation means that the entire universe is implicit in one moment of mental awareness, owing to the interdependence of all things, both mental and material. The second sentence also means that all things in the universe interpenetrate.

6. This is not explained. Perhaps Satomi-san means that the *mappō* teaching explains why she is so bad—everyone is bad in the *mappō* age.

7. The idea of a head being broken into seven pieces may be found in several places in the Buddhist canon, though this phrase is not used in the Buddhist scripture the way this monk uses it. For example, in the *Sutta Nipāta* of the Pali canon there is a story of two Hindu brahmans, one of whom asks the other for some money When the second brahman replies that he has none to give, the first one curses him, saying, "If thou wilt not give to me who asks, may thy head on the seventh day cleave into seven." At this the second brahman is much distressed, but he is comforted by a local deity who tells him that the Buddha has knowledge of the head and head-splitting. The brahman sends his disciples to ask the Buddha about the matter. In reply to their question, the Buddha says, "Ignorance is the head, know this; knowledge cleaves the head, together with belief, thoughtfulness, meditation, determination, and strength." F. Max Müller, gen. ed., *Sacred Books of the East,* 2nd ed. (Delhi: Motilal Banarsidass, 1980), vol. 10, part 2: *The Suttanipata,* trans. V. Fausböll, pp. 176–182.

8. Devadatta was Śākyamuni Buddha's cousin and a monk, but became the Buddha's enemy. He committed the five most heinous crimes according to Buddhism, namely killing one's father, killing one's mother, killing a monk, injuring a buddha's body so that the blood flows, and breaking up the Buddhist order of monks and nuns. Thus he is a symbol of human evil. However, in the *Lotus Sūtra,* Śākyamuni declares that in a former life, he, the Buddha, had been a king seeking enlightenment and Devadatta had been a sage who taught him. The Buddha says it was because of Devadatta's good friendship at that time that he, the Buddha, attained perfect enlightenment. He also predicts that in a future life Devadatta will himself become a buddha. Thus, using Devadatta as a symbol, the *Lotus Sūtra* teaches that all beings, no matter how evil, can attain buddhahood. The Buddha's attitude of gratitude and friendship toward his "enemy" Devadatta, of course, stands in marked contrast to the Nichiren monk's attitude of anger toward his critics.

~ *NOTES FOR PART ONE* ~

7. I FIND A TEACHER

1. "Rō Sensei" is not this teacher's name; it is a title of respect that Satomi-san uses to refer to this teacher (the word *rō* means "old," and age connotes respect). Since Satomi-san uses this term consistently and does not introduce her teacher's name until Chapter 10, I have left the term in the translation. Similarly, "Mrs. Rō" is not the real name of this teacher's wife, but it is the phrase that Satomi-san uses.

2. Shinsendō is a Japanese form of popular Taoism in which the ideal is to train to become an "immortal" who neither ages nor dies, but passes on to a divine world. While living in the ordinary world, such a person would possess mysterious occult powers and would ideally live as a mountain wizard.

3. *Iaijutsu* is a martial art closely related to kendō.

4. A *dōjō* is a meeting place for the practice of religion and arts regarded as fundamentally spiritual, such as meditation, martial arts, tea ceremony, etc.

5. Kannagara-no-Michi Shinto is discussed in detail in Part Two in the section "Religion in the Prewar Era."

6. In Mu kōan practice, one sometimes repeats, "Mu, Mu," out loud while concentrating one's mind on Mu. Satomi-san discusses Mu kōan practice in more detail later in the text.

7. See the section "Mysteries and Marvels" in Part Two for a discussion of this practice.

8. Satori is religious awakening, the attainment of experiential knowledge of the Truth. It constitutes liberation in Buddhism.

8. LEAVING RYŌ-CHAN

1. Kannon Bodhisattva represents the perfection of selfless compassion in the Buddhist tradition. She is one of the most popular figures in Japanese religion.

2. *Namu* means "Hail!" or "Praise to . . . !"

3. Marxism and socialism were often discussed among intellectuals in small study groups such as this one at this time (late Taishō period) in Japan.

4. Tatami are straw mats commonly used as floor coverings in Japan. As they are of a standard size (one tatami is approximately five and a half

by three feet), rooms are measured in terms of how many tatami are needed to cover the floor.

5. Kōans are questions, statements, or dialogues given by a teacher to a student as a means of cultivating or testing the student's religious awareness. One cannot respond to them in a rationally cognitive manner; a different order of awareness is called upon. Kōans are ordinarily used only by the Zen school of Buddhism. The present Shinto kōans are highly unusual.

6. Ō-Kami is not a particular Shinto deity. Rather, this kōan shows the influence of Western thought and means something like "What is God's age and true name?"

7. This reference to the "four spirits" of Shinto touches on an obscure issue. Rarely discussed in ordinary Shinto literature, these four are little understood. They are: (1) *nigimitama* (peaceful or gentle spirit), (2) *aramitama* (rough spirit), (3) *sakamitama* (happy or lucky spirit), and (4) *kushimitama* (marvelous spirit). These four are mentioned in the *Nihonshoki*. The *Kojiki* refers only to the first two. It is a matter of some discussion among Shinto scholars as to whether these are four aspects of a single entity or four separate entities. Satomi-san adopts the former view. In explaining the "one soul" of Shinto, she compares it to the Zen expression "myself before I was born." This refers to the True Self of Zen, which is to be realized in enlightenment experience.

8. The *Kojiki* is the earliest Japanese written document, compiled at court order and completed in 712 C.E. It is a mixture of mythology and history, and is regarded as a classic of Shinto.

9. This man brought this fate upon himself, according to the law of karma. He bound himself mentally and spiritually by his attachment to the matter of the money. At death this act bore fruit when his spirit was bound, in a parallel fashion, by the leg irons.

10. Merit is a "positive" form of karma, which one builds up (much like savings in a bank) by doing meritorious things, such as reading Buddhist sūtras, or sacred texts. This man's wife apparently directed the power of her merit toward helping her husband after his passing from this world. Thus her merit "bore fruit" in the form of releasing him from his suffering.

11. To read sūtras and accumulate merit for her husband.

12. Further weighting the karmic debt toward immediate retribution.

9. A FOOL'S FREEDOM

1. This alludes to the popular Japanese belief that great men (Socrates, Rō Sensei) have bad wives.
2. The reference is obscure.
3. While Kannon Bodhisattva stands on Amida Buddha's left side, representing compassion, Seishi Bodhisattva stands on Amida Buddha's right side and represents wisdom. Wisdom and compassion are the supreme and inseparable virtues in Mahāyāna Buddhism.
4. The six destinies are the six worlds in which sentient beings are born, live, and die and are again reborn according to their karma. The six are hell; the worlds of hungry ghosts, animals, fighting demons, and human beings; and heaven. Note that none of these states, including heaven and hell, is permanent and that birth as a human being is said to be most desirable because it is only as a human being that one can achieve enlightenment and thus true happiness. In Buddhism, the six destinies are sometimes treated as literal places and sometimes as metaphors for states of being.

10. SHINTO SHAMANESS

1. The material in this chapter and the next is considerably rearranged for the sake of clarity.
2. Amaterasu, the "sun goddess," is traditionally the supreme figure in the Shinto pantheon of kami. The word *namu,* meaning "praise to," is usually used in Buddhist chants. Its use here in connection with a Shinto kami exemplifies the syncretic tendency of Japanese religion.
3. According to the Yogācāra school of Mahāyāna Buddhism, "Mind" may be understood in terms of eight *vijñāna,* or principles of consciousness. The first five *vijñāna* correspond to the five senses known in Western psychology. Thus there is an eye-consciousness, which results from the contact of the visual sense organ with the visible sense field, an ear-consciousness, and so on. The sixth consciousness, *manovijñāna,* is in one respect like the first five consciousnesses in that it is the product of the contact of a sense organ (here, reason) with a sense field (ideas). Hence, Buddhist psychology speaks of six senses. *Manas,* the seventh consciousness, is the seat of intellection, emotion, and volition.

    The eighth consciousness, *ālayavijñāna* ("storehouse consciousness"), is something very special. According to the *Laṅkāvatāra Sūtra,* it

is a kind of universal or collective unconscious that acts as the fundamental source or basis of all human experience, both deluded and
enlightened. One way to describe its function is to say that all acts
(karma, including thoughts and feelings) performed by sentient beings
produce "seeds," which are stored in the eighth consciousness until
they ripen or mature, at which time they bear fruit in the form of
consequences of the behavior that produced the seed. Another kind of
explanation (which uses different metaphors but means fundamentally
the same thing) would be that every act we perform "perfumes" or
molds the eighth consciousness in such a way that thereafter there is a
tendency for certain similar sorts of events to result. In this sense, the
eighth consciousness stores memories that subsequently form the basis
for our being conditioned to think, feel, and behave in certain ways.
The eighth consciousness is a transindividual mental principle, and
unconscious. The unconscious memories of all sentient beings of all
time are stored there. (On the subject of this system of Buddhist
psychology, see Daisetz Teitaro Suzuki, *Studies in the Laṅkāvatara Sūtra*.
London: Routledge and Kegan Paul, 1930. Reissued: Boulder: Prajñā
Press, 1981.)

Thus far goes the discussion in Buddhist scripture. Satomi-san's
equation of the eighth consciousness with the "spirit world" is her own
and cannot be traced to the Buddhist canon. Her idea seems to be that
since the eighth consciousness is universal, spirits (which live without
physical bodies in spirit or mental form) must be found there. Since we
all share the same eighth consciousness, trained or sensitive persons
should be able to contact spirits as a natural phenomenon.

4. In this passage, Satomi-san refers to another aspect of this system of
Buddhist psychology, and herein emerges the religious importance of
these ideas. According to the *Laṅkāvatara Sūtra*, the *ālayavijñāna* is
primordially and at all times potentially the seat of perfect enlightenment. In and of itself it is untouched by delusion, error, vice, etc. This
perfectly true and enlightened mind is always present in the depths of
the mind of every sentient being. However, this perfect and clear mind
is concealed by a surface of ignorance and emotions based on selfishness. This deluded mind, which is all that the unenlightened experience, is the product of the sixth and seventh consciousnesses (*manovijñāna* and *manas*) working in conjunction to create the illusion of an
ego. The *ālayavijñāna* is free of all traces of egotism; it is a realm of unity
in which even subject (self) and object (world) are experienced and
known as one. *Manas*, however, divides subject from object and is thus

the most fundamental source of the illusion of an independent ego or self. The religious goal, then, is to effect a radical "turnabout" in the mind, such that one no longer sees only the false, surface mind of the troubled individual self, but instead discovers the deep level of the mind, the *ālayavijñāna,* which is truth itself.

5. This poem and the rest of the chapter return to the theme of the fool, found in the preceding chapter. The idea here is that in recognizing oneself as a fool, one simultaneously recognizes others as wise and capable. Hence the theme of entrusting matters to others follows naturally. Asking for blows is not masochism here, but a poetic device expressing extreme self-negation in the spiritual sense of eradicating egotism.

6. That is, when she loses consciousness of herself as a fool, she begins to behave in a self-centered manner and regrets her behavior.

7. The three evil births are hell, the world of hungry ghosts, and the world of animals. The four evil births are these three plus the world of fighting demons. Here Satomi-san uses these terms metaphorically.

8. All of these are things that *miko* literally may do.

11. POSSESSED BY SPIRITS

1. *Sangaku Buddhism* is a general term for Buddhist sects with the character of mountain cults. The mountain as a center for religious pilgrimage, practice, and worship has a long and complex history in Japan. Mountains were and are seen as sacred in themselves, as the site of sacred events (such as the abode of the dead), and as numinous sites for religious practice, especially of the ascetic and quasi-magical varieties. Included in this category would be some sects of the Tendai and Shingon schools of Buddhism (especially in the Middle Ages) and Shugendō (which will be discussed shortly).

2. A well-known *rōshi* of the Sōtō Zen sect who lived 1839–1925.

3. The "age of the kami" is the mythological period of the acts of the kami, traditionally regarded as prior to the "age of humanity."

4. The *Zazen Wasan* ("Song of Zazen") by the famous Japanese Zen master Hakuin Zenji is a very popular work, chanted daily in many Zen temples and at lay Zen gatherings. A translation may be found in several places, including Isshū Miura and Ruth Fuller Sasaki, *Zen Dust: The History of the Koan and Koan Study in Rinzai (Lin-Chi) Zen* (Kyoto: First Zen Institute of America in Japan, 1966), pp. 251–253; and Trevor

Leggett, ed. and trans., *A First Zen Reader* (Rutland, Vt.: Charles Tuttle Co., 1960), "Hakuin's 'Song of Meditation,'" by Amakuki Sessan, pp. 65–199.

5. *Zazen* is seated meditation as practiced by the Zen school of Buddhism.

6. Shugendō is a popular religious movement which was very influential in Japanese religion from the Heian period to the Meiji Restoration and can still be found today on a smaller scale. It is a mountain cult of a highly syncretic nature, with elements of Buddhist esotericism, shamanism, Taoist magic, and traditional folk religion. Its practices include mountain pilgrimage; the veneration of kami, buddhas, and bodhisattvas; purification; exorcism; magic; and severe asceticism.

7. Human beings originally were and fundamentally are kami. But our hearts (*kokoro*) have become polluted with vice such that we seem far less than kami. When we purify our hearts and free ourselves of pollution, however, we once again fully become the kami that we had been before and potentially are at all times.

8. The Great Purification, Ō-Harae, is a purification ceremony of the Shinto tradition. Certain of its motifs may be traced to a myth of the *Nihonshoki;* its historical practice began in the Taihō era (701–704). It was performed as a biannual event on the last days of the sixth and twelfth months. The officials and imperial attendants gathered at the purification site, the Ō-Harae prayer was read, and the sins and/or pollution of the officials were transferred to "sin bearers" (sticks and reeds) and thrown into the river. By this act, not only the officials but the entire country was purified. The performance of this ceremony gradually declined from the end of the Heian era, and it was discontinued after the Ōnin wars (1467–1477). With the Meiji Reformation in 1871, the ceremony was revived and practiced once again. Not only was it performed by the imperial household, but it also came to be performed annually on June 30 at neighborhood Shinto shrines for the purpose of destroying the impurities accumulated by the local people since the last general purification on New Year's Day. It is also performed by individuals as part of a private religious practice.

9. A self-chosen name. The term connotes a name used in a life of retirement from the world, a life of creative artistic or literary work.

10. This is very much a Zen-style saying, meaning that Truth is to be found in single-minded concentration on and wholehearted engagement in one's daily life.

11. Jizō is the "Earth Store" Bodhisattva, very popular in Japanese religion. He is often depicted in the form of a rough, more or less oval stone stood on end with few or no discernible features. Such stone Jizōs vary considerably in size.

12. A tile, to which Satomi-san compares herself, is a common symbol for something of low value, while both gold and jewels are, of course, valuable and represent the goal to which religious practice leads. Rō Sensei's reply to Satomi-san's question seems to hark back to a well-known Zen story, though Rō Sensei changes the story considerably for his own purposes. The original story is an exchange between Nangaku Ejō, who is the "Master" in the following, and his disciple Baso Dōitsu.

He [Baso] was staying in the monastery of Dembō-in and constantly sat in meditation. The Master knew of his outstanding ability for the Dharma. He came to him and asked: "Excellent one, with what purpose are you sitting here in meditation?"

Dōitsu said: "I wish to become a Buddha."

The Master picked up a tile and rubbed it on a stone in front of the hermitage.

Dōitsu said: "What is the Master doing?"

The Master said: "I am making a mirror by rubbing."

Dōitsu said: "How can a tile become a mirror by rubbing?"

The Master said: "How can one become a Buddha by practicing meditation?"

—Heinrich Dumoulin, *The Development of Chinese Zen after the Sixth Patriarch,* trans. Ruth Fuller Sasaki. (New York: First Zen Institute of America, 1953), pp. 9–10

In the original story, the Master attacks Dōitsu's idea of attaining or becoming "something" through Zen practice. Rō Sensei, on the other hand, wants to encourage Satomi-san's efforts, so in his version, the "rubbing" or "polishing" work of religious practice is unconditionally affirmed.

13. He was evidently to be adopted into the family as heir. This is not uncommon in families, such as Satomi-san's, in which there are daughters but no male heir.

14. The Buddhist term for this world of ignorance in which we wander from birth to death to rebirth until we find enlightenment.

15. In Japanese, *chinkon kishin*. See Part Two, "Encounters with Spirits."

16. The three abdominal areas are the solar plexus, the area of the abdomen above the navel, and the area of the abdomen below the navel.

17. In *gasshō*, one brings the palms of the hands together with fingers extended upward in a way that looks very much like the position of the hands in Christian prayer. *Gasshō* is a sign of veneration. Here, when Rō Sensei offers the prayer to Satomi-san, he is treating her as if she herself were the kami. This is a ceremonial preparation for Satomi-san's possession by the kami: the ritual identification of person and kami is established first, followed by the real identification in the possession experience.

18. This is a term used in Zen as a metaphor for a stage in the Zen student's practice in which "he feels encased in a 'block of ice' or immured in a 'crystal palace.' Now he *virtually* sees the truth, but he cannot break out and take hold of it." In other words, one has almost reached satori, one has in fact a "foretaste" of it, but one is "stuck" and can't quite completely grasp it. (Kapleau, p. 97).

19. Satomi-san evidently feels that her status is ambiguous. Though she successfully passed her public test and successfully served as medium and oracle, she nonetheless failed to secure certification from Rō Sensei and also failed to obtain the "key" to the mysteries of life. Moreover, she feels estranged from her teacher and thus lacks confidence as she proceeds to stand on her own as a *miko*. Even Rō Sensei's parting words emphasize what she still lacks rather than what she has attained.

12. RETURN TO MY VILLAGE

1. The Ontakekyō developed out of a *kō*, or voluntary religious association (a kind of local religious club) which was dedicated to the worship of Mount Ontake in Nagano Prefecture. As it grew and became more organized, it was given the status of one of the thirteen original sects of Sect Shinto during the Meiji period. When this system broke up, it became a fully independent religion, which continues to the present. Given its nature as a mountain cult, it has close ties with Shugendō and with *miko*. Kami possession, the practice of serving as an oracle, and exorcism are all practiced. It is common for independent *miko* to come to the Ontake Church for both advice and training in the arts of the *miko*, no formal ties or lasting relationship necessarily being established.

2. She refers to the concept of *upāya*, meaning skillful means or device. According to Mahāyāna Buddhism, the many words of the Buddha (traditionally cited as 84,000 doctrines) do not contain the Truth as

such, since Truth can only be known experientially and not through words. Thus the teachings of the Buddha are skillful means or devices designed to help people find the way to their own experiential realization of Truth.

3. Fudō is the powerful, wrathful form in which Dainichi Nyorai (the supreme form of Buddha in the Shingon tradition) manifests himself in order to subdue evil. He carries a sword to cut away evil and is usually portrayed wreathed in fire. His enshrinement at waterfalls is indicative of the power of running water to wash away evil.

4. A wrathful form of Kannon Bodhisattva usually portrayed with a horse's head on top of three anthropomorphic faces. In this form, Kannon is the guardian of horses.

5. The "*Kannon Sūtra*" is actually the Kannon chapter of the *Lotus Sūtra*. Cf. Leon Hurvitz, *Scripture of the Lotus Blossom of the Fine Dharma* (New York: Columbia University Press, 1976), chap. 25, "The Gateway to Everywhere of the Bodhisattva He Who Observes the Sounds of the World," p. 318.

6. The ceremony in which the shrine is opened and the chief image is installed. The spirit (in this case, Kannon Bodhisattva) is ushered into the image with the ceremonial completion of the image's eyes.

7. Foxes and raccoon dogs, in addition to snakes, are commonly said to possess people and cause unusual behavior.

8. Traditionally, a Japanese woman was subject to the "three obediences": to obey father, husband, and son or, if she had no son, son-in-law.

9. In the sense of communicating with spirits and developing her rapport with spirits.

13. A HEART FULL OF LONGING

1. With this vow, Amida Buddha guarantees that anyone who repeats his name ten times in sincerity and with faith will be reborn at death in the Pure Land, a Buddhist paradise.

2. Tomomatsu Entai is famous for his teachings on the Indian Buddhist text *Dhammapada*.

3. The father is speaking in a metaphorical way of his daughter. Like the flowers, Satomi-san has lost track of her proper developmental sequence: she has abandoned her family and failed to come to maturity.

4. Sake is Japanese rice wine. The father drank, thought of Satomi-san,

and wept. Koshōgatsu is "Little New Year," a holiday celebrated on about the fifteenth day of the first month on the lunar calendar.

5. The term *New Religions* refers to a large number of Japanese religious groups which developed, for the most part, in this century, especially after World War II. Several of them have very large followings. As a group, they are extremely powerful in the religious life of contemporary Japan. See Part Two for further comments.

14. KNOCKING AT THE GATES OF ZEN

1. All famous collections of kōans.
2. Bodhidharma is the traditional first patriarch of Zen and a favorite subject in Zen art.
3. The room set aside for *zazen* practice.
4. The *hara* is the lower abdominal region. In *zazen* practice, one is often told to concentrate all of one's energies in the *hara* and to put one's mind in the *hara,* because it is believed to be a center of mental and physical energy.
5. In Buddhism, to leave home represents the severing of karmic bonds, i.e., the severing of attachment to delusion and self-interest. Śākyamuni Buddha established the model by leaving the comforts and pleasures of home to search for religious truth.
6. The six perfections are six kinds of practice in which Mahāyāna Buddhists engage. They are: giving, keeping the Buddhist precepts, endurance, effort, meditation, and wisdom.
7. Hīnayāna Buddhism, the so-called Lesser Vehicle, and Mahāyāna Buddhism, the so-called Great Vehicle, are the two great traditions into which the Buddhist world is divided. By "Hīnayāna-type giving vow," Satomi-san means a vow to give things in a literal sense. Satomi-san hopes that by practicing the perfection of giving, the sixth perfection, wisdom or enlightenment (her goal), will also be achieved.
8. This is because she would be reborn with the same karma from which she wanted to escape.
9. Amenominakanushi-no-Ōkami was one of the kami in the ancient Japanese pantheon as recorded in the Japanese classics. In the Restoration Shinto of Hirata Atsutane (1776–1843), this kami is elevated from a rather obscure position to become the creator god of the entire universe, all-powerful, all-knowing, and eternal. Understood in this

way, this kami never became an object of widespread personal faith, presumably because of its philosophical, otherworldly character, which is quite alien to the native Japanese tradition.

10. Dew drops and dust are symbols for this world of evanescence and delusion. According to Zen philosophy, everyone possesses the innately pure Buddha nature, or own-nature. This means that all have the potential to attain enlightenment. Once enlightened, one can see that this world, which appears contaminated with the dust of hatred, greed, ignorance, etc., is in fact pure and always has been.

15. SICK OF CHASING SATORI

1. The poems are given at the end of Chapter 14. A *waka* is a poem composed of thirty-one Japanese syllables.
2. In a culture, such as Japan's, which values age, this is a polite thing to say and not in the least rude or insulting.
3. The three poisons are greed, anger, and delusion.
4. The ten worlds are the ten states of existence of living beings: beings in hell, hungry ghosts, animals, fighting demons, human beings, and heavenly beings; *śrāvakas, pratyekabuddhas,* and bodhisattvas (three categories of Buddhist saints); and buddhas.
5. Serious practitioners of Mahāyāna Buddhism vow to save all sentient beings before they themselves attain final enlightenment or *nirvāṇa*.

16. "I CAN'T DIE BEFORE MAKING YOU BUDDHAS!"

1. At that time, six years.
2. *"Ga-te, ga-te"* are Sanskrit words left in the original language in the Japanese translation of *The Heart Sūtra*. They are a mantra; that is, truth and power are said to be present in the words themselves, rather than in anything to which they refer. The text is a short rendering of the Buddhist "perfection of wisdom" teachings, and the mantra is the essence of that teaching.
3. Satomi-san is referring to the following interchange between the Zen masters Huang-po (Japanese: Ōbaku) and Lin-chi (Japanese: Rinzai), recorded in the Chinese Zen text *The Transmission of the Lamp:*

> One day after half the summer session had already passed, Lin-chi went up the mountain to visit his master Huang-po, whom

he found reading a sutra [Buddhist scripture]. Lin-chi said to him:

"I thought you were the perfect man, but here you are, apparently a dull old monk, swallowing black beans [Chinese characters]."

—Chang Chung-yuan (ed. and trans.), *Original Teachings of Ch'an Buddhism* (New York: Random House, 1969), p. 119.

4. A bodhisattva, in Mahāyāna Buddhism, is one who is on the way to becoming a buddha and has vowed to put off his or her own final enlightenment until all beings have been liberated from suffering. A bodhisattva, therefore, is ideally a completely selfless, altruistic being. Hayakawa-san questions Satomi-san's motivation in planning to set herself up as a teacher.

17. DHARMA FRIEND

1. This exchange harks back to the kōan "Hyakujo and a Fox," found in the *Mumonkan*. Hayakawa-san appears to use this kōan in the right spirit. Cf. Shibayama, pp. 33–42.

2. Satomi-san's discussion of self and own-nature refers to the Mahāyāna Buddhist teaching that all things lack self or own-nature insofar as every entity exists as the temporary, constantly changing product of conditions outside of itself with no unchanging core or essence that constitutes its basic identity. Nonetheless, it is paradoxically stated that insofar as it is the essential nature of a thing to lack this essence or self, one may truly say that the self (essence) of a thing is not-self. Thus true self is not-self. Satomi-san depicts herself as parroting this kind of language without really understanding it.

3. This is Mahāyāna Buddhist philosophy. It means that enlightenment is to be found directly in everyday life, just as it is.

4. It is not moving in the sense that there is nowhere to go; the Truth for which one searches is to be found right here, right now. Yet insofar as one does not yet see it, one moves ahead in search.

5. Shinshū is the school of Pure Land Buddhism founded by Shinran (1173–1262). Shinran initiated many changes to laicize Buddhism.

6. In one kind of lion dance, the dancer, wearing a lion's head costume, dances from house to house, accompanied by flute, drum, bells, etc., asking for rice and money.

18. TWO CRACKS IN THE RICE PAPER

1. That is, there are as many as two cracks in the veil of illusion that prevents her true, enlightened nature from shining out.
2. One's own real treasure is the true self. To find this is the goal of Zen.
3. Heaven-and-Earth is the universe. Here and in the following paragraph Satomi-san calls up the associations of the Confucian *Doctrine of the Mean,* in which Heaven-and-Earth is a cosmic power with which one attains unity through one's sincerity.
4. Literally, "Leaving home [as a monk or nun] is *kenshō* ['seeing the self']; staying home [as a layperson] is *monshō* ['hearing about the self']." The Buddhist scholars with whom the translator spoke also said they had never heard of such a thing as *monshō*. The statement is not representative of Mahāyāna Buddhist thought.

19. KNOCKING OVER FLAGPOLES

1. A formal talk given by a Zen Rōshi.
2. The private interview with the Rōshi in which the student presents his or her mind for examination.
3. An illusion produced by the intense mental effort of meditation.
4. The kōan reads, "Ananda once said to Kasho, 'The World Honored One [the Buddha] transmitted to you the brocade robe. What else did he transmit to you?' Kasho called out, 'Ananda!' Ananda answered, 'Yes, sir.' Kasho said, 'Pull down the flagpole at the gate.'" (Shibayama, p. 164)
5. That is, she determined to maintain the concentration of psychophysical energy in her lower abdomen, which was to be used as energy for meditation.

20. JOY

1. In prolonged *zazen* sessions, a period of walking meditation is interspersed with rounds of seated meditation.
2. The spirits of deceased persons are enshrined on the "spirit shelf"; they are believed to inhabit that area.
3. Cf. Matthew 7:7.
4. This is a reference to a well-known legend. One day an old woman who was irreligious and greedy was hanging clothes out to air when a

neighbor's ox ran by and caught the clothes on its horns. Chasing after the ox without realizing where it was leading her, she followed it into the nearby Zenkōji Temple. When she realized that she was in a spiritual place, she made a prayer for the next life. Moral: Even a chance event may in the end lead to good consequences.

5. Amida Buddha practiced Buddhism for aeons in order to acquire the capacity to save humanity—not human heroes, but ordinary, confused people. Though this quotation from Shinran (and Satomi-san's subsequent statement) may appear egocentric, it is in fact the opposite. It is an expression of overwhelming gratitude for an utterly undeserved gift:

"The Master [Shinran] used to say, 'When I carefully consider the Vow which Amida brought forth after five kalpas' contemplation, I find that it was solely for me, Shinran, alone! So how gracious is the Original Vow of Amida, who resolved to save me, possessed of many karmic sins!" (Ryūkoku University Translation Center under the Direction of Ryōsetsu Fujiwara, *The Tanni Shō: Notes Lamenting Differences* [Kyoto: Ryūkoku University, 1962], p. 79)

6. The first five syllables of Satomi-san's poem are the same as the first five syllables of her teacher's poem.

7. Satomi-san seems to have in mind the founders of certain New Religions who claim to be the abode of the Divine and are called "living kami" by their followers.

8. According to legend, this is what Śākyamuni Buddha cried out at birth. Another translation might be: "I shall be the all-honored one throughout heaven and earth."

9. Powers that most people lack but that are felt to be the natural accompaniment of profound meditation practice.

10. That is, if that person is not utterly free of self or, in other words, enlightened.

11. The *mani* jewel fulfills all wishes. It symbolizes enlightenment, which fulfills humanity's true desire.

12. According to Zen, enlightenment is a matter of freeing the mind; it is not a matter of acquiring anything at all.

13. Grasshoppers represent the dead. "Shadows of the grass" is a euphemism for "graveyard."

PART TWO

Commentary

The World of Satomi-san

SATOMI MATSUNO (Buddhist name: Satomi Myōdō) was born and raised in a small farming village in central Hokkaido, the northernmost of the four principal islands that constitute Japan. Though situated on the outskirts of the largest city in Hokkaido, Sapporo, it remains even today rural and quiet, buffered by its location well into the mountains. Hokkaido is in many ways unlike the main Japanese island, Honshu, with which foreigners tend to be more familiar; it has a far shorter history as part of the Japanese nation and cultural unit. Earlier inhabited by a separate racial and cultural group, the Ainu (who indeed once inhabited most of the land area of Japan, but were pushed farther and farther north by the Japanese), Hokkaido was only opened up to active colonization from the more southerly Japanese islands in 1868, when it was formally made part of Japanese territory. Thus the long history and deeply engrained traditions of a place like Kyoto are not so important in Hokkaido. Even today, the area claims something of a frontier spirit. Hokkaido, moreover, is far less densely populated than the more southerly islands. In the latter, even farming villages seem crowded to an American, with houses clustered together in small areas to leave the maximum possible space for the fields. In Hokkaido, the fields themselves are larger and the houses scattered individually among them, leaving considerable distance between one family's home and the next.

In such a place, Satomi-san, an only child, was raised. Intelligent and independent, with dreams of becoming a writer, she was sent to Tokyo, then as now the "big city," a good place for the ambitious to go. Soon, however, Satomi-san's impetuous and rebellious spirit got her into trouble and she had to return home. From that time on, her life became one of both spiritual and physical wandering. At home in both town and country, she traveled to Tokyo, Nagoya (a large city on the main island), and Shikoku (one of the four main islands of Japan, relatively undeveloped and rural). She lived in each of these places more than once, but spent by far the greatest number of years in her native Hokkaido and her second home, Tokyo.

Satomi-san was born in 1896, the twenty-ninth year of the Meiji era by Japanese count. She died in 1978. Her life thus spanned a period of tremendous social, political, and religious change in Japanese history. I shall first give a brief overview of the social and political changes that took place during this period; the religious history of the period is treated in a separate discussion.

The Meiji era is recognized as the dividing line between feudal and modern Japan. The Meiji Restoration in 1868 marked the formal end of rule by the Shōgun-headed feudalistic government and the simultaneous restoration of the emperor to supreme political authority. Much more was involved, however, than the mere replacement of one head of state by another; the Restoration ushered in a fundamentally new form of government. Feudalism was replaced with a modern, centralized administration in which the emperor and his cabinet ruled as executives, while the elected legislature struggled to influence policy despite its initially limited powers. The period was one of rapid modernization, encompassing industrialization, urbanization, and the importation of Western ideas and influence. Indeed, a crisis over Japan's relations with the West had helped to bring down the feudal government, which had maintained a policy of national isolation for centuries. When the new government opened the nation's doors to the West, a barrage of new ideas came flooding in. Thus, while the Meiji leaders looked to the past in returning the emperor to a supreme position, they very much looked to the future in building commerce, international trade, and a modern army.

When the Meiji leadership ended Japan's isolation and confronted the Western powers, they found that they were very much at an economic and military disadvantage vis-à-vis Europe and the United States. Thus one of the ambitions that drove these leaders was to transform Japan as quickly as possible into a modern state that could meet the West on terms of equality. The Western powers had initially demanded unequal trade agreements with the Japanese, to which Japan was forced to accede. This, plus Japanese observation of Western expansion in Asia (a powerless China was then being virtually carved up and distributed among the Western powers) and a clear sense of Japan's own economic and military weakness, acted to steer the minds of Japan's policymakers to the subsequent course of action: rapid economic and military development. The Japanese feared what the West might do to them if they did not quickly achieve a position of equality with the Western powers.

As a result, two general policies were followed: (1) the Japanese rushed to import Western ideas and technology for the development of Japanese political institutions, the educational system, commerce, agriculture, and the military, and (2) intense efforts were made to develop a strong nationalistic sentiment among the people while strengthening the military and building an economy capable of supporting a nation at war. Significant progress was made in both areas with quite remarkable speed.

Though the central government instigated these moves, in the end it was not able to control them fully. With the people becoming more and more indoctrinated in nationalistic and ultranationalistic thought, largely by means of the state educational system and conscription into the military, popular sentiment turned toward antiforeign feelings and the desire for international adventurism and expansion. The army, in turn, was so successfully strengthened that its leaders began to initiate foreign campaigns without the direction or even the permission of the central government. In effect, though the initial push may have come from the government, the military machine began to roll on its own inertia, backed by intense emotional support from the people. The result was three wars: with China (1894–1895), with Russia (1904–1905), and World War II (1937–1945); the first two were remarkably successful, the latter, of course, disastrously unsuccessful, for the Japanese.

In short, the period from 1868 to 1945 saw Japan throwing off feudalistic government and achieving a modern government, economy, and society, along with ever-greater nationalistic and expansionist sentiment. The defeat in 1945 ushered in another set of sudden changes for Japan. By the end of the war, Japan was an economically drained nation, the war effort having taken everything its land and people could give. With defeat, the people's spirit too was drained. The Allied Occupation (1945–1952), controlled by the United States under the direction of General Douglas MacArthur, brought rapid economic recovery and significant political and social changes, notably complete demilitarization, the virtual elimination of the power of the Imperial House, and a constitution drafted by the Occupation authorities, with power transferred squarely to an elected diet headed by a prime minister. Japan became independent of foreign control only in April 1952. The Japanese "economic miracle" of the postwar period brought affluence, stability, and self-assurance to the Japanese.

Though this dramatic period constitutes the historical context for Satomi-san's life, we see little direct comment on these matters in the text. Her only direct reference to Japan's wars, for example, occurs at the end of Chapter 15. Depressed and spiritually lost, she envies those persons whose bodies she sees stretched out dead on the floor of the train station, victims of starvation. This is just before the end of World War II, when there were severe food shortages in Japan. In an indirect reference to Japanese expansionism in this period, she speaks in Chapter 14 of a Mr. K_____ who had just returned from Manchuria (then a Japanese colony that the Japanese government was encouraging its citizens to populate) and who was living in a state of utter poverty.

Such references as these are rare, but we may gather from other evidence that the influence of the times on Satomi-san's life was far from negligible. For example, when Satomi-san, early in the story, suffers a complete nervous breakdown, her hallucinations involve the image of Fujimura Misao. Fujimura committed suicide in 1903, leaving behind a suicide note declaring: "Life is incomprehensible." Indeed, life was incomprehensible for many Japanese of the Meiji and Taishō eras (1912–1925), who were torn between an old order and way of life, by no means dead, based upon traditional Confucian, Buddhist, and Shinto ideas, and a new order, not yet entirely formed, in which one heard first of democratic individualism, then of nationalism, then of Marxism. Political, social, educational, and family institutions were all in the throes of change. On what values was one to base one's life? Life appeared to be built on a shifting sea of sand. Fujimura Misao was to many in the late Meiji and Taishō eras a symbol of the times: his world was in such an uproar of change that it became intolerable, and he sought escape in suicide. It is remarkable that when Satomi-san's life becomes intolerable and she seeks escape in temporary insanity, her mind calls up the image of this man. It may not be too much to suggest that in this instance her subconscious reveals (with its choice of hallucinatory image) that her personal crisis is based not only on the specific events that she narrates, but perhaps also in a general way on the crisis of spirit endured by all the Japanese of the time.

A second factor demonstrates in an undeniable manner the influence of the times on Satomi-san's life, namely, her practice of a form of Shinto called Kannagara-no-Michi. This phenomenon is sufficiently complex, however, as to require separate treatment in the following section.

Religion in the Prewar Era

During the Tokugawa period (1600–1867), the school of Koku-gaku, or National Learning, developed in Japan with the aim of promoting the study of the Japanese classics. For centuries, because of the overwhelming influence of Chinese culture (especially Confucianism and Buddhism) in Japan, the Japanese classics had been either overlooked or lost in interpretations based on Chinese traditions. The Kokugaku school used new linguistic and philological techniques to recover the ancient texts and to try to determine their original meaning. Along with this scholarly aim went an emotional desire to discard all corrupting, alien influences and return to the "pure" Japanese content. Thus the school had marked antiforeign and national-istic sentiment. The members of the school tended to believe that what was Japanese was good and what was foreign was bad. They thoroughly rejected Confucianism and Buddhism and wanted to pare these influences away from Japan's own national tradition, Shinto.

In the late Tokugawa and early Meiji periods, Kokugaku ideas came to dominate the Shinto world. A form of Shinto called Kannagara-no-Michi developed in this period as one interpretation of Kokugaku thought. Ostensibly this was a "pure" Shinto, devoid of Buddhist and Confucian accretions. "Kannagara-no-Michi" was interpreted by its adherents as an-other name for Shinto in the sense of the Japanese national tradition. According to this perspective, Shinto is the path peculiar to Japan that has been handed down from the primordial age of the kami (according to the Japanese classics, this is the ancient age when the kami—the Japanese gods—created Japan and lived in it) to modern times, and maintained as the Japanese way of life.

Kannagara-no-Michi teaches that in ancient times the human heart was perfectly in accord with the kami heart. Thus the kami will was the human will, naturally and spontaneously. Effortlessly, all lived in natural harmony both with the kami and with each other. This, however, was the golden age of the ancient past. In modern times, such harmony was no longer evident. To return to that condition of naturalness and harmony was the aim of Kannagara-no-Michi; the very name was interpreted to mean "behaving in accordance with the will of the kami." To follow this path was to put aside all human will and desire, hence all artificiality, and to live with one's heart and behavior fully and naturally in accord with the will of the kami. Pure human behavior was seen as an expression of the state of being of the kami, a manifestation of the true nature of the kami. This, it was believed, was the ancient tradition of Japan and the source of Japan's greatness. To this, it was urged, Japan should return, putting aside foreign ways.

Kokugaku thought was not limited to such nationalistically shaded religious ideas, though; it also encompassed distinctive religiously colored political teachings. Members of the Kokugaku school concluded, by means of their study of the ancient texts, that the emperor, and not the shōgun, was rightfully the supreme ruler of Japan. They also taught, on the basis of the ancient classics, that the Japanese emperors were not mere human beings, but living kami, direct, lineal descendants of the great heavenly kami, Amaterasu, the "sun goddess." This concept also became part of Kannagara-no-Michi teachings. Thus, in line with this understanding, "behaving in accordance with the will of the kami" could be understood as simply obeying the emperor.

One Kokugaku scholar who greatly influenced both the political and religious worlds was Hirata Atsutane (1776–1843). Hirata, who was one of several major Kokugaku advocates of Kannagara-no-Michi, is known as the systematizer of the Restoration Shinto school of Kokugaku. This school had considerable influence on the Japanese intellectual world of the time, significantly shaping the climate of thought that made possible the restoration of imperial rule with the Meiji Restoration of 1868. While the Kokugaku school and its Restoration Shinto version were not political movements as such, their tenets were easily applied to political ends. Though both taught that the emperor and imperial ancestors should be worshiped, as befits any kami, neither turned veneration of the emperor into an attack on the shōgun. In a relatively short time, however, Hirata's teachings spread among those who were interested in overthrowing the shōgun. Some feudal lords even changed the official ethos of their domains from Confucianism to Kokugaku. These people found that Hirata's teachings served their needs as an ideology for the hoped-for new regime.

Hirata's books were censured by the Tokugawa government, and he was sent into exile, where he died. His movement, however, continued to grow and influence subsequent events. This was the period just before the Meiji Restoration when the feeling was growing in Japan that Westerners were a threat and that the shōgun-headed feudalistic government should be overthrown and replaced by a government based on restoration of imperial rule. A political movement spearheaded by the slogan "Revere the emperor and expel the barbarians" (i.e., foreigners) grew more and more powerful. Restoration Shinto gave an ideological foundation to this movement.

When the Meiji emperor came to power, many significant religious changes were instituted, in addition to the political and social changes mentioned above. Restoration Shinto heavily influenced the nature of these religious changes. Generally speaking, during the Tokugawa period, the state had supported Buddhism and used it for its own ends. For example, every family had been required to belong to a Buddhist temple, where such things as births and deaths were registered. With the Meiji Restoration, the ideological grounding in Restoration Shinto led to a complete reversal of this policy, resulting in the disestablishment of Buddhism, coupled with state support and use of Shinto.

The Meiji leaders experimented with a number of forms of relationship between the government and Shinto. One of the slogans that symbolized the early Meiji period was "Unity of religion and government." In accordance with Kannagara-no-Michi tenets, the emperor was regarded as the descendent of the kami Amaterasu; thus he himself was a living kami, head of what could be seen as a theocratic state. He was simultaneously the supreme political and religious figure. The religion that was in unity with the government was Kannagara-no-Michi; it was officially promoted from the throne. The following are excerpts from imperial edicts of the first three years of the Meiji era.

> Reverence to the gods and regard to the [Shinto] ritual constitute the proprieties of the Empire and are the fundamental principles of the National Polity and Education.

> From the very day our Great Ancestor [Amaterasu] undertook the establishment of the Empire she paid homage to the gods, and treated her subjects with tender affection. The origin of "the unity of religion and state" lies far back.

At this time the Heavenly Course of the Nation has turned, and thus all things are become new. By all means, polity and education should be made clear to the Nation, and thus the Great Way of *Kannagara* should be promulgated. Therefore preachers shall be ordered to propagate the Way far and wide.[1]

In its first attempt to institutionalize the unity of religion and government, the Meiji government created a Department of Shinto, establishing it as the highest government office. Conversely, Buddhism saw its governmental backing entirely taken away, with such measures as government confiscation of Buddhist lands and transfer of the public registry function from Buddhist temples to Shinto shrines. As shown in the third quotation above, the government hired preachers to promulgate Kannagara-no-Michi among the population. Hirata Atsutane's followers were prominent among the architects of such policies as these.

In time it became clear that Buddhism was too firmly entrenched among the Japanese populace to be extirpated by such measures. Moreover, it proved impossible for government bureaucrats to create and foster a religion that could satisfy the people. In addition, demands from Western nations that Japan adopt a policy of religious freedom (Christianity having been banned) became difficult to ignore. The government finally adopted a policy according to which religious freedom and the separation of state and religion were declared. However, this pronouncement did not match the state's actions. Certain religious functions, such as the performance of funeral ceremonies, were stripped from what was now declared to be "nonreligious" State Shinto. The government continued to support Shinto under a new guise, and Shinto priests were charged with performing "nonreligious" national rites based on Shinto tradition. The principles of morality and nationalism taught in the public schools continued to be based on a mixture of Kannagara-no-Michi thought and traditional Confucian ethics stressing loyalty and obedience. Other religions were theoretically free but in fact were carefully controlled and often suppressed by the state.

Given this context, it is quite remarkable that although Satomi-san specifies Kannagara-no-Michi as the form of Shinto which she studies, there is not a single reference to nationalistic teachings in the entire text. This is perhaps best explained by pointing to the gulf that inevitably existed between government bureaucrats pushing the ideas found in Kokugaku, Restoration Shinto, and Kannagara-no-Michi for political purposes and ordinary people studying and practicing these traditions for their own personal ends. It was quite possible for a person such as Satomi-san to practice Kannagara-no-Michi privately for purely religious reasons even though in the public domain the tradition was heavily laden with political content. She could, and evidently did, simply ignore the political aspects of the teachings, in which she had no interest, and concentrate on the spiritual aspects, which served her needs well. Quite aside from any political considerations, Satomi-san's concern, and that which she portrays her teacher as having, is to become a person capable of living fully in harmony with the true nature of the kami.

Writing in 1938, the great scholar of Japanese religion Masaharu Anesaki says of the Shinto taught in this period: "Its chief feature is the teaching of patriotism centered on the sanctity of the throne and the inculcating of the virtues of loyalty and filial piety. This 'visible,' namely, ethical and political, side is supplemented by the 'invisible,' or religious and mysterious, side."[2] Anesaki goes on to list the kinds of practices that constitute the "invisible" side of the religion, providing a list of precisely those practices that Satomi-san details in her work: purification by cold-water bathing and breath control, exorcism, chanting, and the like. These are seen as part of the "pure" Japanese national tradition of Shinto, though in fact they are better understood as deriving from Japanese popular religion in which Chinese and Japanese practices from several traditions have been blended. Thus Shinto teachers such as Satomi-san's taught a version of Shinto that perhaps gave lip service to the political ideas so stressed by the state, but concentrated on popular religious beliefs and practices of mixed ancestry with deep, long-standing popular acceptance. It is the "invisible" side of Kannagara-no-Michi that Satomi-san shares with us.

Kami, Buddha, Bodhisattva

The Japanese religious landscape is filled with many kinds of divine beings, three of which concern us here: kami, buddha, and bodhisattva. Ostensibly kami belong to the Shinto tradition, while buddhas and bodhisattvas belong to Buddhism. In practice, although these distinctions can readily be made, they are often not so significant as we might expect. The Japanese tradition is thoroughly infused with a syncretic spirit and history, such that during Japan's medieval period, Shinto and Buddhism virtually merged in theory and in practice, while today one almost never encounters a sizable Buddhist temple without a Shinto shrine on its grounds. Most traditional-minded people respect and venerate both.

What is a kami? The Shinto tradition is one that is more in touch with mood and emotion than with rational clarity. As a result, a precise definition of kami is not to be found, though this does not mean that a Japanese person doesn't know what a kami is. As the contemporary Shinto authority Sokyo Ono says, the Japanese people "are aware of the kami intuitively at the depth of their consciousness and communicate with the kami directly without having formed the kami-idea conceptually or theologically."[3] The kami with which they commune are to be found virtually everywhere: for example, an island, rock, tree, or mountain may be a kami; there are "heavenly" kami whose exploits are recounted in the mythological sections of the Shinto classics (*Kojiki* and *Nihongi*) and whose shrines are found scattered throughout Japan; emperors are all kami, as are some military heroes, religious leaders, and various "great" persons; many a field houses the shrine of the kami of agriculture, or a snake or fox kami. In general, it should be noted that this is not an organized or controlled system. If a number of people regard a natural phenomenon, a person, or an animal as a kami, then that phenomenon, person, or animal is a kami. Anything capable of producing a strong emotional response in people— anything unusual, awesome, striking, impressive, powerful, beautiful, or fearful, anything that seems more wonderful than the ordinary—may be regarded as a kami. Thus kami are exceedingly numerous, their shrines found in every neighborhood and community. New kami continue to be recognized today, notably among persons who are the founders of New Religions.

Buddhas and bodhisattvas are the embodiments of wisdom and compassion. A buddha is a completely and perfectly enlightened being, with enlightenment understood primarily in terms of wisdom (i.e., knowledge of the true nature of things) and compassion, or selfless benevolence toward all living beings. Though there are many buddhas, the most important for Satomi-san's text are Śākyamuni and Amida. Śākyamuni is the historical founder of the Buddhist tradition, the only historical figure among all the buddhas. He lived in Northeast India in approximately 560–480 B.C.E. and experientially discovered the truth which he then taught. Amida Buddha is a non-historical, cosmic buddha best known for his vows to save all beings from suffering if they will but turn to him.

Bodhisattvas are much like buddhas in that they represent wisdom and compassion, but in practice they are felt to be less remote than the tremendously awesome buddhas. A bodhisattva is a manifestation of a particular quality or function of a buddha. The two most popular bodhisattvas in the Japanese tradition, Kannon and Jizō, are both loved for their compassionate actions on behalf of humanity. Kannon Bodhisattva, often called the Bodhisattva of Compassion, stands at the left side of Amida Buddha in the traditional iconography and is universally popular throughout Japan. Her very name indicates that she sees and hears all that happens and is ready to respond instantly to anyone in distress who calls on her. She is depicted in many forms: one form, with eleven heads, depicts her ability to look and listen in all directions at once; another, with a thousand arms, manifests her ability to help in infinite ways simultaneously. Her powers are limitless. In particular, it is said that she saves those who suffer in fire, disasters at sea, and floods, those pursued by ghosts and demons, and those attacked by sword or by thieves, and that she can assure safe and easy childbirth. She is popularly felt to have a benevolent attitude, much like a loving mother.

Jizō Bodhisattva, the "Earth Store" bodhisattva, is another compassionate figure whose task it is to help suffering beings in the period between the last historical buddha, Śākyamuni, and the advent of the buddha who is expected next to live on earth, Maitreya. In the interim period, during which there is no buddha on earth to teach humanity (i.e., the present), Jizō Bodhisattva is here to help. In particular, his association with the earth makes him known for helping travelers and those in hell (the underworld). He is especially venerated for protecting the spirits of dead, miscarried, and aborted children. The latter function involves him in a very emotional cult. His statue is often found clothed in baby bibs or knitted caps, or again he may be depicted with babies and young children in his arms or at his feet.

Kami, buddhas, and bodhisattvas clearly have individual characters and functions, but they have an important quality in common: they all demonstrate the immanence of the sacred.

Kami, buddhas, and bodhisattvas are all sacred beings, yet they are all very much present in the world, involved in human struggles, and are, in fact, very similar in their nature to the "true nature" of human beings, if not identical. This immanence of the sacred is expressed in a variety of ways. Kami manifest the sacredness of the land of Japan and of life itself. Furthermore, as mentioned above, people may be regarded as kami if they express special qualities or demonstrate great achievements in life. Buddhism, for its part, teaches that the ultimate goal of human life is to become a buddha or bodhisattva. One reads repeatedly in the Buddhist texts that there is fundamentally no difference between a buddha and an ordinary human being, that we share the same intrinsic nature. Satomi-san wants to maximize this promised closeness between herself and the sacred world of kami, buddha, and bodhisattva. This is done in two ways: by removing those qualities in herself that separate her from kami, buddha, and bodhisattva, and by looking deep within herself to discover her true nature, which is said to be one with the nature of kami, buddha, and bodhisattva.

Makoto and Kokoro

The concept of *makoto,* translated in the text as "sincerity," is at the very heart of Shinto. *Makoto* is both the fundamental spirit that the Shinto tradition hopes to express and a state of being that the faithful hope to realize. The concept of *makoto* is closely linked to that of honesty or truthfulness. In addition, its connotations include genuineness, integrity, and the completion or perfection of the individual. Yamakage Motohisa lists four "pillars" of Shinto: purity, clarity, truthfulness, and uprightness; these four taken together, he says, constitute the foundation of *makoto.*[4] To be sincere is to be true to the total situation in which one finds oneself; that is, to be true to oneself (or one's true nature) and the kami, in addition to one's neighbors. Here we encounter the fundamental optimism of the Shinto tradition and especially of the *makoto* concept: it is possible to be true to all of these at once. There is no fundamental conflict between one's own needs and those of others, between the immediate demands of a complex world and the aspirations of one's ideals. The faith inherent in the *makoto* concept is that if one is truly *makoto,* or sincere, one will be so deeply in harmony with the true nature of all things that one will effortlessly do what is right. What is right for one is right for all; this is what it means to be "true" to the situation, or sincere. Thus *makoto* points to the individual engaged in the community as much as to the individual's personal self-cultivation. In fact, the former is the necessary extension of the latter.

This aspect of the *makoto* concept takes us to the Chinese Confucian tradition and the *Doctrine of the Mean*, attributed to Confucius' grandson, Tzu-ssu. The text was early introduced to Japan and thoroughly assimilated into the Japanese culture. Regarding sincerity, the text has the following to say:

> Only those who are absolutely sincere can fully develop their
> . nature. If they can [do this] . . . they can then fully develop the
> nature of others. If they can [do this] . . . they can then assist in
> the transforming and nourishing process of Heaven and
> Earth. . . . [Able to do this] they can thus form a trinity with
> Heaven and Earth. . . . It is characteristic of absolute sincerity
> to be able to foreknow . . . calamity or blessing. . . . Therefore
> he who has absolute sincerity is like a spirit. . . . Sincerity is
> the beginning and end of all things. Without sincerity there
> would be nothing. . . . Sincerity is not only the completion [or
> perfection] of one's own self, it is that by which all things are
> completed [or perfected].[5]

Though this quotation is taken from an ancient Chinese text, it represents a perspective very close to Satomi-san's way of thinking. In the Confucian view, sincerity is as basic to the structure and function of the universe as anything else one can name. It is built into the very fabric of the universe and functions in an invariable, predictable, and reliable fashion. What's more, the ancient Chinese saw the universe as an organic whole, in which all parts are intrinsically interrelated. This being the case, sincerity is not only a cosmic principle, but also a principle of nature and of humanity. Thus, insofar as we are intelligent beings, we may come to know and understand this sincerity, which orders not only our lives but the very universe as well. Thus, in Confucian language, by fully realizing sincerity, we develop our own nature and that of others, and, in harmony with the great powers of Heaven-and-Earth, take part in the very processes that govern life itself. Sincerity, then, is not just a virtue in the limited sense of the word. It is a power, a power capable at the least of transforming human lives, and ultimately of much more.

Satomi-san's introduction to sincerity comes from her father, who, very much in the spirit of the above quotation, uses his own sincerity to "develop" Satomi-san's nature. Once she becomes aware of the reality of sincerity, her life as a spiritual seeker begins; sincerity frees her from misery and opens up her spirit. She now wants to "develop" others, by using her own sincerity to teach others the reality and value of a moral and religious life. She is as optimistic about the unlimited potential of sincerity as the author of the *Doctrine of the Mean*. "I believed without a doubt that sincerity could raise the dead," she writes.

One important aspect of *makoto* peculiar to the Japanese tradition is the idea that it is common to both kami and human beings. The link between the two is *kokoro. Kokoro* is a single thing, but its meaning incorporates what we understand as two things: the human heart and mind. (Thus, in the translation, it is sometimes rendered with one term and sometimes with the other.) *Kokoro* is the seat of emotion, intellection, and the human spirit or psyche in general. It should, however, be distinguished from "spirit" in the sense of a nonphysical life principle that survives death; that is also a reality for Satomi-san, but it is something else.

As we have seen, the line between human beings and kami is not an absolute or inviolable one; human beings may be or become kami. Even apart from these exceptional cases, though, human beings in general are regarded as being very closely related to kami; the crucial, linking factor is a *kokoro* that is *makoto,* a heart that is sincere. The following two poems express that close connection between a sincere heart and the kami. The first is by Sugawara-no-Michizane:

If your heart is on the path of sincerity,
the kami will protect you, even if you don't pray.[6]

Makoto is shared by person and kami; there is no need for anything further—such as prayer—to connect them. Second, a poem by Emperor Meiji:

The sincerity of the human heart
penetrates to the invisible kami heart itself.[7]

Again, a direct link, here from human *kokoro* to kami *kokoro* by way of *makoto*. Finally, we might cite a Japanese proverb that expresses a similar idea using the term *shōjiki*, or "honesty," a close synonym of *makoto*. The proverb reads, "Kami lives in the heads of the honest."[8]

What this means for Satomi-san is that ultimately the human *kokoro*, when it is sincere, and the kami *kokoro*, which is always sincere, are the same. By becoming a sincere person, one returns to one's original and true nature and simultaneously discovers, as Satomi-san says, "I am kami; just as kami is in itself, so am I." Thus, to be sincere is to know one's true nature, which is the same as one's kami nature. Here we encounter once again the fundamental optimism of the Shinto tradition: not only is human nature basically good, it is divine. To realize that divinity, however, requires effort, which in Shinto means purification.

Purification

Some say that Shinto "begins and ends" with purification, or *harae.*[9] It might be more accurate, however, to say that while both Shinto and Japanese popular religion in general begin with purification and are permeated by purificatory practices, the hoped-for end is a state of purity. As we have seen, the goal of religious practice is to return to one's original nature, a sincere heart, which is identical with the kami nature. This sincere heart is absolutely pure.

As human beings our birthright is this pure, kami-like heart, or *kokoro.* With the passage of time and the difficulties of life, however, this originally pure heart has become tainted with pollution. We have become estranged from the kami and our better selves. A variety of purificatory practices have therefore been developed in the Japanese tradition to rid us of this acquired pollution and thus allow us to return to our originally pure and sacred condition.

Exactly what the nature of pollution is, is a matter of some discussion. Certainly a strong case can be made to support the position that pollution in this tradition is regarded as a physical thing, like germs or something unclean that approaches a person from outside and becomes fixed to the body. With such an understanding, a physical cleansing is needed to rid one of physical pollution. Thus the ancient prayer of the Great Purification (Ō Harae) effects a purification or exorcism of the pollution resulting from such things as improper agricultural practices, skin diseases, and sexual misconduct. The pollution is transferred from the afflicted person to pieces of wood and reed, which are then thrown into the river.[10]

It is also clear, however, that by modern times pollution can no longer be understood in purely physical terms. Satomi-san provides an example. She feels at a certain point that her Zen practice is not progressing as she expects it should. "What is this all about?" she asks herself. "It must be because I've got some impurity left in a corner of my heart. The first thing I've got to do is find it and get rid of it." What she finds after a search is selfish stinginess, clearly not a physical pollution, and this, she decides, is the impurity preventing further progress in her religious practice. Thus impurities may have an internal, "moral" or "spiritual" nature or an external, "physical" nature. For the religious seeker, all of this must be purged in order for the religious quest to succeed. Impurity is a barrier to progress on the Way.

Many practices are used for the purpose of purification in the Japanese tradition. Here I will speak only of those in which Satomi-san engaged. First, there is the general category of *kugyō,* painful or difficult practices, that is, asceticism. As Carmen Blacker says of them, "In so far as they are painful, exhausting or wearisomely repetitive, in so far as they remove both body and mind from their accustomed habits, in so far as they require very great strength of will to accomplish, they may properly be described as ascetic."[11]

Varying degrees of asceticism may be found in the religious traditions of Japan; Shugendō (a tradition of magic and asceticism associated with mountain cults) is perhaps best known for extreme asceticism. Of general ascetic practices, Satomi-san notes that she fasts and limits her clothing to a single unlined kimono. Fasting, of course, is an ascetic technique known throughout the world. The object of fasting in Japan, however, is not to weaken or break down the body—the body as such is by no means inherently evil or of negative value in Japan—but rather, to purify oneself of any pollutions attached to the body. It should also be noted that a second object of this and other ascetic practices is the acquisition of spiritual power. It is accepted as a simple matter of fact that one who engages in ascetic discipline will develop as a natural result a variety of spiritual powers, such as concentration, communication with the spirit world, and the ability to cure disease. Satomi-san herself attests to the power of ascetic practice to bring about such results, as we shall shortly see. Her practice of limiting herself to a single unlined kimono was one in which she engaged during the winter months, thus by an act of will refusing to protect herself from the cold. (The traditional Japanese home is neither heated nor built so as to keep the cold out.) This too is thus an ascetic practice, with the aim of developing spiritual power.

One particular form of ascetic practice that carries especially great prestige and enjoys widespread practice in Japan is *misogi,* and Satomi-san engages in it to a very considerable extent. Basically, *misogi* is purification by cold water. Many sources of water are used: the ocean, a river, a waterfall, or a simple bucket of water. Satomi-san mentions engaging in *misogi* practice in a river and by using a bucket; in many other cases, *misogi* under a waterfall is particularly prized. *Misogi* may be performed nude or clothed (in a white loincloth for men, a white robe for women). If one is practicing *misogi* with a body of water such as ocean, river, or waterfall, one first washes the face and genital area, then enters the water. Men submerge themselves entirely three times, while women are asked to go in only up to the neck. One then recites a purificatory prayer such as the Misogi prayer or the Ō Harae prayer. One may then leave the site or repeat the prayer and submersions any number of times. In the case of using a bucket, the procedure is similar, with bucket after bucket of cold water being poured over the head and body, interspersed with the recitation of prayers.

Such a practice is believed to result in the two benefits noted above: purification and the acquisition of spiritual powers. To the extent that pollution is believed to be a physical thing, cold-water bathing is a practical means of removing one's acquired impurities. But *misogi*, as it is popularly practiced, goes far beyond a simple physical cleansing into the category of asceticism. Especially with the emphasis on performing the ablutions at the coldest time of year and the coldest hours of night, with many repetitions and over long periods of time, *misogi* can become ascetic indeed.

Satomi-san describes in some detail one such practice in which she engaged. Beginning in the coldest part of the winter, she leaves a bucket of water out overnight to freeze; at dawn, she breaks the ice and pours the water over herself. Afterward she sits outside, naked, practicing meditation. She does the same thing again the last thing at night. She continues this practice until spring, when the arrival of warm weather makes it impossible to continue. As a result of this practice, Satomi-san becomes a physical wreck, apparently suffering hemorrhage, and wonders, with hindsight, that she didn't kill herself.[12] But, she says, as a direct result of this ascetic practice, communication with the spirit world opened up and she began to be capable of performing as a *miko*.

For Satomi-san, there is a direct equation between the degree of purity that she attains by virtue of her ascetic practices (including *misogi*) and her personal spiritual progress. She notes, "As might be expected, during the period of ascetic practice, with my body purified, deluded thoughts had no chance to put in an appearance." There is fundamentally no mind-body dualism in the Japanese tradition, as we see here. A pure body means a pure mind, and vice versa. When she notes a flaw in her character or moral behavior, Satomi-san simply concludes that she needs more ascetic practice, more purification. Thus pollution has both mental and physical qualities, and the *kokoro,* or heart, which in the final analysis is what most essentially must become pure, is likewise of an indivisibly psychophysical nature.

A final important form of purification in which Satomi-san engages is purification of the breath.[13] Her Shinto teacher emphasizes these techniques as the foundation of his teachings, saying that they put both body and mind in good order. Note again the psychophysical nature of this practice. Buddhism is well known for stressing the effects of breathing techniques on the mind, and here Shinto follows suit. Certain breathing techniques calm body and mind and hence develop clarity of mind and concentration. Others generate psychophysical energy, which can be directed toward the goal of religious practice.

Satomi-san's teacher refers to breath purification as "the act of the kami," saying that the breath sweeps away all one's faults and impurities and sends them "to the far side of the ocean." Here it sounds as if the kami are external to the one practicing breath purification and descend on the practitioner to remove the pollution. Certainly there is a tradition in Japanese religion that would understand the process this way: without the intervention of the kami, any purificatory exercise is fruitless. Satomi-san's teacher also says, however, that in the act of practicing breath purification, one is expressing, "I am kami; just as kami is in itself, so am I." Here kami and practitioner are identical. It may be best to avoid thinking of these two forms of expression as conflicting. To the extent that one experiences oneself as polluted or impure, then one is separate from kami, the sacred. But to the extent that one experiences one's heart and mind as clear and pure (for example, when successfully performing the breath purification practices), then one is no longer separate from kami; one has returned to one's originally pure *kokoro,* which is identical with kami.

Specifically, what techniques of breath purification is Satomi-san taught? In addition to certain unspecified preliminary breathing techniques, she mentions a "heavenly breath" and a "deep chant." The former involves sitting Japanese style in *seiza* (on one's knees with a straight back), closing the eyes and repeating "oo-oo" with intense concentration for an hour or more. This is clearly a practice designed to promote calm and intense concentration, as the mind becomes concentrated when a single thing—here the "oo" sound—is attended to, rather than several. It also presumably leads the practitioner into an altered or trance state of consciousness (the constant repetition of a single sensory stimulus may often bring this about). The "deep chant" consists in chanting over and over again the vowels of the Japanese alphabet in mixed order with all of one's energy, breath, and voice. This is evidently an energizing practice, as well as one conducive to an altered state of consciousness (due to hyperventilation and sensory repetition). It should also be highly purificatory, in the sense that vast quantities of air are taken into the body and expelled.

With the techniques of asceticism and purification, in particular those of breath purification and cold-water ablutions, Satomi-san engages in a struggle to become perfectly sincere and to acquire spiritual powers. These two ends are interwoven in her practice with no apparent sense of discrepancy. This makes sense in the context of the Japanese tradition, for sincerity is not just a perfect state of being, it is power, a power capable of "raising the dead." Such a spiritual power as communication with the spirits of the dead belongs here most logically. Sincerity should be capable of this and more. Moreover, a sincere heart is the kami spirit, and the kami are nothing if not spiritual powers. Sincerity and purity are identical, and both entail the acquisition of power.

Women in Japanese Religion

I will limit my discussion in this section to two topics: the *miko*—her nature, history, and craft; and the role played by gender in Satomi-san's religious life. We will begin with the *miko*. The Japanese word *miko* means "shamaness" (*ko* means "female"); this, then, is a tradition dominated by females. Satomi-san was a *miko* for many years; the way of the *miko* was one of the two main paths she took in her search for spiritual liberation.

The *miko* is a figure of considerable importance in Japanese religions, especially in the "little" tradition. This term requires explanation. Scholars of religion distinguish between "great" and "little" religious traditions. The terms are not meant to impute greater or lesser value to one tradition or another. Rather, a "great" tradition is institutionalized religion: a religion with a name, such as Christianity or Buddhism; a clear identity that distinguishes and separates it from other religious traditions; a written scripture; professionals who perform the "business" of the religion, its rituals and teaching; characteristic holy buildings where the religion is practiced; and so on. A "little" tradition is popular or folk religion. It is much more difficult for the outsider to know, for it is based on an oral rather than a written tradition. It encompasses the folk beliefs, legends, customs, traditions, and festivals of the common people, handed down as a way of life rather than as a doctrine or an "ism," from generation to generation. It is unorganized and uncontrolled, both a molder and an expression of the everyday life, feelings, and beliefs of the people.

There are two general types of *miko* found in Japan today, one in the great and one in the little tradition. The first may be called a shrine *miko*. She is a girl or woman who serves in a Shinto shrine, performing a variety of tasks in a secondary role of assistance to the priest (usually male) who holds the position of authority in the shrine. A shrine *miko* will do such things as perform special sacred dances called *kagura* (ostensibly to please the kami of the shrine, though the public also enjoys the dance); sing sacred songs; assist in all sorts of rituals and cere-monies, including weddings; and help clean the shrine and shrine precincts. This kind of *miko* is very numerous and, as part of institutionalized Shinto, very visible. This is not the kind of *miko* with which we are concerned here, however.

The second major type is the shamanic *miko*—the kind of *miko* that Satomi-san was. There are many kinds of shamanic *miko,* but generally speaking, this is a woman who belongs to the little tradition. She possesses the ability to enter at will into a state of trance for the purpose of communicating with resi-dents of the "other world": kami, spirits, and the deceased. In her trance she is possessed by a kami or spirit who speaks through her mouth to those assembled. In this way the kami or spirit reveals its will, and humanity is made capable of respond-ing. Often the kami or spirit, through the mouth of the miko, will speak of the future, predicting the weather, the farming or fishing harvest, the coming bad or good fortune of the commu-nity or the individual. Again, the *miko* may summon the spirit of a deceased ancestor who will convey to the family his or her wishes and perhaps speak of what the future will bring them. The *miko* may also summon a spirit who has possessed someone and thereby caused illness or other suffering. Through the *miko,* the spirit will reveal its identity and needs and then be exorcised from the sufferer. By performing such functions as these, the miko provides a unique and indispensable service for her community.

In ancient times, the official status of the shrine *miko* and the power of the shamanic *miko* appear to have been located in a single individual. Sources on the ancient *miko* are few, but it seems that in late prehistoric Japan—that is, before Chinese culture, including religion, philosophy, statecraft, and a writing system, came to Japan—the shamanic *miko* was a powerful person who served at the highest level of the state. Most famous is the Japanese queen Himiko (or Pimiko), who ruled over thirty Japanese states from 180 to 240 C.E. and of whom an account is recorded in the chronicles of the Chinese Wei dynasty:

> . . . the people of Wo [the ancient Chinese name for Japan] elected a young girl as their queen who was then named Himiko. She attended and rendered service to the Deities or Spirits and had a special power that bewitched the people. She never married even in her youth, and her brother helped her administer the affairs of the Kingdom. After she was enthroned, only a few persons were able to see her.[14]

Queen Himiko ruled by virtue of her shamanistic powers and charismatic personality; it was these that gave her the support of the people and the ability to rule. As in numerous other cultures, in many prehistoric Japanese states it was believed that the best ruler was one who had close rapport with the gods and derived power from them. Queen Himiko is the paradigmatic example of such a ruler. It is difficult to state with confidence how many other female rulers there were in ancient Japan before the many small states of the several islands were consolidated to form the Japanese nation. Though legend and history are woven together here, tradition has it that there were many shamanistic female rulers in Japan in ancient times.

There are also many instances in the ancient sources of emperors with shamanistic consorts. The best-known case is that of Emperor Chūai and Empress Jingū, chronicled in the *Kojiki* and *Nihon Shoki*. According to the *Kojiki* account, the emperor, empress, and chief minister entered the sacred enclosure of the *saniwa* to question the kami about an intended attack on the natives of Kumaso.[15] On this occasion, the empress served as medium, the emperor as musician, and the chief minister as questioner. The empress became possessed and through her the kami advised an attack on an unknown land to the west, rather than the Kumaso attack. The emperor angrily denounced the kami for lying, as there was nothing to the west but the sea. For this he was cursed by the kami and struck dead. The counsel of the kami was later found to be reliable; the land was Korea and the Japanese invasion was successful. Here we see the empress clearly using the kind of shamanic power that appears today on a far humbler level among the village *miko*. In ancient times, such powers were commonly required by the rulers of the land—either in the person of the ruler herself or, in the case of males, in one close to the ruler, his consort, sister, or niece, for example.

With the coming of Chinese culture from the mainland, Japan underwent revolutionary changes that affected virtually every aspect of the traditional culture and every segment of society. Though, again, sources are few, scholars surmise that the radical decline of the position of the *miko* from the highest social standing to the most humble is related to this importation of Chinese culture. This process crystallized with the Taika Reform of 645 C.E., which was undertaken with the intention of remodeling the Japanese state after that of the Chinese T'ang dynasty. Confucianism was adopted as the new state ideology and was used to unify Japan under a strong, central male emperor. Two elements of Confucianism that inevitably adversely affected the high standing of the *miko* were its male supremacism and its rationalism. No longer could a female possibly be head of state. Nor could shamanistic powers, with their attendant loss of rational control, establish a claim to secular power. From this time on, the status of the *miko* declined. As the old system broke up, the official *miko* disappeared from government service. Some *miko* became the shrine *miko* we see today, maintaining official positions of respect (though religious, not secular) but losing virtually all their shamanistic powers. Others became entertainers—singers, balladeers, and the like—adapting the talents and techniques developed in their previous calling; these also lost their shamanistic power. A third group, however, maintained this ability to mediate between the gods and humanity. Descending into the little tradition and practicing shamanism among the common people, these *miko* handed down their tradition orally and informally, with no established doctrinal or institutional framework. As a consequence of this eschewal of lasting records and structures, their history is difficult to discern, but the shamanic *miko* still practices her craft today. Though her numbers have been reduced since the Meiji Restoration, people still depend on her special abilities, especially in the more remote areas of Japan.

Satomi-san's early life and character in many ways follow the typical pattern of the shamanistic *miko*. She demonstrates in her youth that she possesses a good measure of intelligence, firm determination, and considerable spunk. She is self-reliant and nonconformist and utterly rejects what she sees as the hypocritical values of her community. Her society tries in vain to mold her into the standard female type being pushed at the time, the "good wife and wise mother." She will have none of it, dreaming instead of independence and self-expression as a writer. Her rebelliousness leads her into rash behavior that results in her becoming pregnant. This event leads to others—

marriage, parenthood, loss of child—which leave her deeply grieving and mentally unstable. Sorrow built upon sorrow, coupled with self-isolation and grand dreams, eventually lead her to a complete nervous breakdown and institutionalization in a mental hospital. While still in a transitional state between sanity and insanity, however, she experiences numerous dreams, visions, and auditions, including a divine command to go out and put an end to the evil of the world.

All of this, in its broad outlines, is typical of the *miko:* a strong, intelligent, and independent personality, coupled with rejection of her society's values and expectations. More often than not, the *miko* experiences conflict with society's expectation that she will marry and, in accordance with the ideal model, settle into a submissive and obedient wife. Typically (though there are exceptions) the *miko* rejects marriage or marries unhappily and becomes an unsatisfactory wife. Often one who becomes a *miko* suffers the loss of dear ones, such as children, and consequently is deeply grieved. Of particular importance is the mental-emotional instability of the future *miko*. One major type of shaman-to-be found throughout the world experiences "initiatory sickness." Though this may result in a variety of symptoms, usually the initiate hovers in an unstable mental condition halfway between sanity and insanity; the initiate hears and sees things, dreams prophetically, babbles in strange tongues, and wanders about in delirium. This syndrome represents the breaking down of the ordinary state of consciousness, a necessary preliminary to the shaman's gaining access to the other states of consciousness that take hold in shamanic trance and divine possession.

From the perspective of the average person, when the ordinary state of consciousness breaks down, sanity and contact with reality are lost. From the perspective of the shaman, when the ordinary state of consciousness breaks down, one state of consciousness with access to one aspect of reality is moved aside to make way for another state of consciousness with access to another aspect of reality. The "initiatory sickness" is an unstable period, when the future shaman does not yet have control over the new state of consciousness that is becoming available. Traditionally, the one experiencing the symptoms of initiatory sickness received the training of a shaman, thus gaining control over the new state of consciousness, the ability to enter it at will and to interpret the meaning of the information it makes accessible. Satomi-san, as a modern, was taken away to a mental hospital during this period and "cured"; that is, she returned to an ordinary state of consciousness. However, though the hospital "cured" her, the underlying unhappiness and dissatisfaction that originally led to her nervous breakdown were left untouched. It remained for her, a few years later, to open up once again this nonordinary state of consciousness, but this time in a controlled way, under the tutelage of one who could help her develop this potentially dangerous ability. Thus in Satomi-san's case, as for many shamans, the initiatory trauma and mental instability served to nurture the power of a *miko*. Like many another religious figure, the *miko* must die to the old to be born to the new.

An important aspect of the *miko* that remains to be discussed is the fact that her role is fundamentally one of service to her community. Mircea Eliade has stressed this point with regard to the shaman generally, and it holds for the *miko* as well.[16] It is ironic that early in life the *miko* must experience conflict with her society and its expectations, making possible her break with the ordinary way of life and the state of consciousness of the average person, only to return in the end to her community and serve it, now from the position of one with special powers valued by that community. Though the *miko* presumably derives considerable personal satisfaction and fulfillment from her role, she does not enter into trance seeking divine possession to have her own questions answered. It is members of her community who ask questions and receive answers, communications from the deceased, or exorcism. The *miko* is a professional; her profession is service. Once trained, she is completely independent; her success or failure depends entirely on her ability. One who is capable, however, should have no problem succeeding as a *miko*—at least until modernization turns potential customers away from such traditions. As Satomi-san said, "When I worked as a *miko,* business really thrived."

Let us now consider what effect Satomi-san's gender had on her life as recorded in the present text. Satomi-san's experience and life is in many respects what it is because she is a woman. She herself traces the beginning of her troubles to the lectures to which she was regularly subjected in her youth on the theme of becoming a "good wife and wise mother," lectures that she found degrading. Later she does marry and bears two children. She is unhappy, though, and wants to divorce her husband but refrains, thinking, "There could be no excuse for making [the children] orphans, come what may." In her view, and in that of her society, a fatherless child is an orphan—her status as mother is that negligible. In due course her husband leaves her anyway, and she is left with complete responsibility for the two children. No arrangements for the welfare of the children were made by her husband before or after his departure. At this point, her mental condition begins to seriously deteriorate. Certainly her abandonment and the weight of responsibility she bears for the children contribute to this, if they do not altogether cause it. In an unstable mental condition, she travels to Tokyo with one of the children, hallucinations and grand dreams filling her mind. In order to study, she leaves the baby alone in her apartment while she attends classes. While some of us may pass over the husband's abandonment of the children without a pause—this sort of thing being done all the time in the arbitrary assumption that the woman bears the greater responsibility for the child (even though a fatherless child is called an orphan)—few will be able to pass over Satomi-san's behavior in leaving the child alone for hours on end. Without attempting to excuse or condone her behavior in any way, it nonetheless should be stressed that this is her confused and insufficient response to a problem she faces because she is a woman. Her husband got out of the marriage and on with his life by simply walking out the door. Left with two children, how is Satomi-san to get on with her life in a society completely lacking in baby-sitters, day care, nursery schools, or other forms of child care (outside the extended family)? She struggles with the dilemma and fails utterly, losing child and sanity as a result.

Years later, sanity restored, Satomi-san becomes a *miko*—an almost inevitable choice, given her gender and temperament. Yet even as a mature woman and a fully qualified *miko*, financially independent and working hard for the good of her community, Satomi-san still thinks in terms of the restraints placed on her because of her sex. Looking back to the time when she was deeply involved in trying to improve the fortunes of her village, she writes, "At that time Father's health was poor and my son-in-law was reserved toward me. Thus, for the most part, I was able to act as my own mind directed." Being a woman, Satomi-san felt constrained by the traditional Confucian concept of the "three obediences" that a woman owed to father (as a child), husband (when married), and son (after the husband's death). Satomi-san was an unusual woman in that she was free of these constraints, her father being old and ill, her husband having left her, and her son-in-law (as she had no son) being withdrawn and reticent. Hence, she was able to be her own person, rather than belong to the men of her family.

These, of course, are only a few of the specific effects on her life that can be traced to Satomi-san's gender. They can only begin to hint at the total effect on her life of such a basic factor as gender. Of course, it was not her femaleness as such that was responsible for these events (except insofar as she bore children), but her gender in the context of her culture's views on women. As we have seen, these views had a largely negative impact on her life. She was the one left fully responsible for the children, despite the fact that a fatherless child was considered an orphan. Particularly telling is the fact that she was at all times to obey the males of her family; even as a grown woman she should have obeyed her son-in-law. Her accomplishments despite such constraints (to which all Japanese women were, and to a large extent still are, subject) are all the more remarkable.

Bearing in mind the above, we may point to two factors in Japanese culture that partially mitigate the power of the generally negative views of women and women's consequent second-class status in that society. The first factor is the existence in the little tradition of Japan of the culture of the *miko*. In this tradition, women's spirituality bears fruit. As a *miko*, Satomi-san was completely independent and responsible to herself alone. She held a position valued by her community in a profession of service.

The second factor helpful to women is the strong thread of optimism regarding human nature that runs through the two main religions of Japan, Shinto and Buddhism. As we have seen in the discussion of *makoto*, in Shinto the human heart is held to be fundamentally pure and ultimately divine: "I am kami; just as kami is in itself, so am I." A similarly optimistic view of human nature is taught in Zen Buddhism (and will be discussed below): your nature is Buddha's nature. Such teachings as these tell women that even though their society treats them as second-class citizens, they are ultimately identical with the kami and buddhas. It is true that the institutional forms of these religions can and do perpetuate the second-class status of women: though in the modern period both traditions have engaged in efforts to reform themselves in this respect, historically both traditions have largely (though with some important exceptions) excluded and/or subordinated women in a systematic fashion.[17] Nevertheless, the philosophy discussed above is egalitarian. It has an impact on women's lives despite the nonegalitarian institutions that convey it. This is clear from Satomi-san's narrative. The strenuous purification practices in which she engages while training to be a *miko* presuppose that she can become pure; otherwise, she would not put herself through so much effort. Her teacher himself tells her, when she is discouraged, that if she works hard, she will become a magnificent jewel, a treasure for the world. Her continual striving, despite repeated setbacks and disappointments, must be traced both to her indomitable spirit and to the optimism of the philosophies she followed, which promised her, respectively, that she was kami, she was buddha, and if she just worked hard enough and kept trying, she would realize this for herself. One Zen teacher promised, "I can't die before making you into buddha." In the context of such optimistic philosophies, and with the encouragement of her Shinto and Zen teachers, Satomi-san does keep on struggling, despite repeated blows. Again and again she speaks in the following vein: "As long as I have breath . . . I will push straight ahead, despite mountains, despite rivers! If I fall down, I'll get up again! If I stumble, I'll right myself! Just advance! Just advance!" She keeps striving both because she refuses to be defeated and because the teachings which she follows assure her that she, the concrete, historical, flesh-and-blood woman that she is, even with her personal shortcomings and blemished past, is certainly pure kami, perfect buddha.

Encounters with Spirits

The world of popular Japanese religion teems with spirits of all kinds: benevolent, malevolent, and mischievous; human, animal, and kami; the spirits of dead and of living beings. Any of these spirits may come into contact with a human being in a number of ways and with a variety of results. To begin with, let us survey the territory. A spirit may simply appear to a person or it may possess a person. Possessions, in turn, may come to a person spontaneously or a person may seek them. Sometimes when a person who has not sought such an encounter is possessed, the person may experience symptoms of disease, personality disorders, hallucinations, or other undesirable or painful afflictions. In such cases, exorcism may be called for, to force the intruding spirit to leave the victim's body, thus bringing relief from the symptoms. Again, when a person, for example a professional *miko*, seeks possession, she usually desires one of two things. First, she may wish to be possessed by a benevolent kami or the spirit of a deceased person, in order to transmit the words of the kami or deceased to her client. Second, as the medium in an exorcism, she may wish for the spirit afflicting another person to be transferred to her, so that the spirit's identity and concerns can be made known and the exorcism effected. Examples of all these types of encounters with spirits may be found in Satomi-san's text, to which we now turn.

First, let us consider the cases in which spirits appear to Satomi-san without possession. Her experience by no means exhausts the variety of possible spirit encounters, but the cases she cites are typical of some of those possibilities. Of course, many people would speak of these phenomena as hallucinations rather than as cases of spirit encounter, and in fact Satomi-san experiences a number of spiritual visions and voices that she herself is prepared to label as hallucinations. Nonetheless, there are others that she is not prepared to understand in this way. Even after she converts to Zen, which generally does not attribute much of value to such experiences, she finds she cannot dismiss these things, but must take them seriously and try to make sense of them. Let us look at some specific instances and try to see them through Satomi-san's eyes, understanding them as she does.

There are three cases in the text in which Satomi-san sees spirits without becoming possessed. All three involve spirits of the dead, one animal and two human. In the first case, the author relates that she had been feeding and caring for an abandoned dog for some time when he suddenly disappeared. Three days after his disappearance, the spirit of the dog, who had died, visited her. As he stood before her, his shocking appearance made clear what had happened to him: he had been killed. This visit put an end to Satomi-san's wondering and worrying about him. In another case, Satomi-san reports that she was followed around for days on end by a mysterious spirit. She finally decided this had to be the spirit of her common-law husband's deceased mother. Satomi-san believed that the spirit was worried about what would happen to her son if Satomi-san left him, as she was indeed planning to do. She spoke to the spirit in earnest, trying to put the spirit's mind to rest. As she was speaking, the spirit's form vanished and never appeared again. The third case is the most dramatic and the most difficult to explain by natural means. Satomi-san relates that she was visited by the spirit of a man who had recently died. He told her that he had been confined after death in a "gloomy, narrow place," shackled in leg irons. He explained his condition to her and the reason for which he had been sent to such an unhappy place—on his deathbed he had been thinking about the money someone owed him. He wanted Satomi-san to tell his wife that he had been freed from this dark and unhappy place thanks to her (his wife's) spiritual devotions. When Satomi-san related the story to the wife, the latter confirmed all the details in such a way as to indicate that Satomi-san could have had access to no other source of such information than her deceased husband.

Satomi-san herself is quite convinced of the authenticity of all three episodes. Of the dog's visitation she says, " 'This is no dream . . . even though he really has been killed and has had his hide skinned off, the dead Koro took on his old form and came to me!' I couldn't help crying." She also feels strong emotion when encountering the dead woman's spirit: " 'Oh, how painful for her! A young mother—even in the other world she must be terribly concerned about her children! She must be overcome with worry for Ryō-chan to appear before me like this!' . . . I was in earnest; I certainly couldn't try to gloss over a ghost's concerns!" Of her encounter with the spirit of the dead man, she says firmly and unequivocally, "I saw the figure clearly. (And I believe that this was neither a hallucination nor an optical illusion.)" These judgments are maintained from the perspective of many years' hindsight and spiritual experience of considerable depth and variety. Certain other experiences she is willing to question or dismiss; these remain valid in her mind.

Although all of these experiences occurred before Satomi-san became a professional *miko*, it is precisely in order to obtain communications like these from deceased relatives that people often turn to *miko*. Spirits, however, may desire on their own part to communicate with living human beings. Though the "spirit world" is spoken of as distinct from the world in which we live, it is nonetheless very close to our world, and the spirits who live there may be quite deeply involved in the events of our world, especially in matters concerning family and past events—wrongs that the spirit wants to avenge, favors that the spirit wants to repay, or thwarted ambitions or desires that the spirit wants to enjoy vicariously through another. It appears to be a relatively easy thing for a spirit to enter into the world of human beings, though ordinarily there must be a specific motive of the sorts mentioned to move a spirit to actually reach out. As Satomi-san said of the dead woman's spirit, "She must be overcome with worry for Ryō-chan to appear before me like this!" On the other hand, human beings, understandably, are not always willing to quietly accept the visitations of spirits. Even if a spirit wants to reach out to a living human being, the latter must cooperate if there is to be any communication. Satomi-san writes that when the spirit of the deceased man appeared to her, "I firmly calmed myself down until my heart became as still as an ocean without a single, tiny wave." It was after she succeeded in calming herself that the spirit began speaking to her.

Since this form of cooperation is not always possible, two other forms of spirit-human communication are common. In the first, the spirit again is the initiator in acting to possess a person. In the second, a person seeks communication with a kami or spirit by seeking possession. (I leave prayer out of consideration here, though it too is, of course, a form of communication between a human and a spiritual being.)

There are two examples in the present text of spirit-initiated possession. First, at the very end of the book, when Satomi-san is working very hard and on the verge of achieving the spiritual enlightenment for which she has been seeking all her life, a final obstacle blocks her way: in the middle of an intensive meditation retreat, her efforts at meditation are repeatedly spoiled as she is pulled over onto her back by a mysterious, invisible power. Finally she determines that she is being possessed by the spirits of the deceased who are enshrined in the temple where she is meditating. She speaks to them, telling them to wait quietly until she has attained enlightenment, after which she promises she will perform a memorial service for them. With this, their obfuscating presence is withdrawn, and Satomi-san is able to break through at last to enlightenment.

In this incident, Satomi-san believes that the spirits are reaching out to her, in effect, to get her attention. She responds by acknowledging their presence and effectively agreeing that she should pay more attention to them and will do so in the future. This appears to satisfy them, as they withdraw. In this case there was no verbal communication from spirit to human; the physical communication was sufficient for Satomi-san to get the message and respond in a way that satisfied the spirits' mute demands. It is clear that Satomi-san felt they were making a request of her—why else would they approach her and pester her until she responded? To offer a memorial service—consisting of offerings of food, candles, incense, etc., in a religious service—is perhaps the most common way to pacify the spirits of the dead and hence a natural response in a case such as this in which the spirits do not make specific requests.

In the second case of spirit-initiated possession, a girl named Yoshida-san is possessed by the spirit of a snake. According to her tale, she had been walking home from school with a group of children one day when they happened upon a snake in the middle of the path. Yoshida-san watched as the other children beat it and slit open its body. Seeing Yoshida-san's pity, the snake spirit leaped from its body at the moment of death onto Yoshida-san. This, of course, was unknown to Yoshida-san. The snake spirit dwelled in her body for many years until finally, at the age of forty-nine, Yoshida-san became afflicted with a strange disease that no one was able to cure. Three years after the onset of the disease, Yoshida-san asked for exorcism.

In this case, the context of the spirit-initiated possession is one of violent death. In Japanese religion one often encounters stories of violent or unjust death resulting in restless spirits, both in animals and humans. Here the suddenness, the pain, and perhaps especially the cruelty involved all contribute to making this death unlike a natural death. A spirit's condition after death is greatly affected by the manner of death. A peaceful, natural death generally results in a peaceful spirit that goes on its way, leaving behind the world of the living. A sudden and violent death leaves the spirit still attached to the world of the living. In this case, it is interesting that the spirit is attracted to the girl who feels pity for it; the spirit declares that it wants to go on receiving her warmth and compassion. It does not, as is often the case, want to seek revenge on those who killed it. All the same, as usual, it has a clear and strong motivation to initiate possession.

The physical suffering that Yoshida-san experiences as a result of the possession led her finally to seek exorcism. Before the exorcism, of course, she had no idea that she was possessed by the snake or what the reason was for the possession. Other means having failed, however, she turned to exorcism as a last resort. This brings us to our first case of human-initiated possession and to our only instance of exorcism. In order for the exorcism to be carried out, someone must become possessed by the spirit that is possessing the afflicted, in order to ascertain its identity, nature, and wishes. Here, Satomi-san serves as the medium, becoming possessed by the snake and allowing her body to be used as an instrument for the snake to reveal itself.

Satomi-san and her teacher perform the exorcism together, as is often the case today, with Satomi-san acting as the medium who becomes possessed and speaks the spirit's words, and her teacher helping to bring about the possession with his chanting and ritual, and then questioning the spirit when it appears. After Satomi-san enters a state of trance, her teacher chants the Descent of the Spirit spell, and Satomi-san's hands rise above her head in a movement indicative of spirit possession. The spirit who possesses Satomi-san is the snake who had possessed Yoshida-san for so many years. The snake tells its story through Satomi-san's mouth. At the end it describes a small and neglected shrine in a nearby field and says that it can be found there. It asks that Yoshida-san give offerings to it at that shrine so that it can continue to receive her warmth and compassion.

With this the exorcism is effected. The identity of the possessing spirit, its motivation for possessing, and its present wishes have all been determined. Such an understanding is necessary for an exorcism to take place. Knowledge, as is often the case in magical or quasi-magical practices, is power. In this case, an understanding of the spirit and its wishes enables one to satisfy those wishes. The spirit will now peacefully leave Yoshida-san's body, and her symptoms should disappear. But she must continue to share her feelings of compassion with the spirit or risk another possession. In effect, though Yoshida-san's body is free of the spirit, she is still involved with it and will continue to be so all her life. Now, however, she can deal with the spirit more on her own terms, rather than on the terms it dictates from its position of control in possession. She can return to health and a fully normal life, visiting the shrine regularly to offer flowers and to let the snake spirit feel her presence and feelings of compassion.

The ceremony of which this particular exorcism is a part is called *chinkon kishin,* Pacification of the Soul and Return of the Kami. Let us digress here briefly to consider this ceremony.

Ceremonies with this name are found in many forms and variations in the Shinto and Buddhist traditions and in the New Religions, historically and at present. Moreover, one often encounters the *chinkon* (also pronounced *mitama shizume*) by itself. This is a very ancient practice, again found in many variations. In one form it was performed as a ritual for the emperor, with the objective of lengthening his life. His spirit was tranquilized or pacified so that it would remain in his body and he would remain alive. In another form, it is performed as a ritual to pacify the spirit of the recently deceased. For several days after death, it is believed, the spirit remains in the home. It is important during this period to pacify the spirit, inducing it to accept its new status and leave the world of the living behind, going on to the world of the spirits. Both these forms of *chinkon* are rituals performed with the aim of pacifying the spirit of another.

Another form of *chinkon* approaches the kind of thing Satomi-san does. This *chinkon* is performed as a religious discipline rather than as a ritual. There are two purposes to it: to pacify one's spirit and to induce the kami spirit to enter one's body. The first aim, the pacification of the spirit, is effected for Satomi-san in the *chinkon kishin* which she relates to us by her teacher, who chants the Pacification of the Soul spell, after which she enters into a state of trance characterized by absolute stillness of body and mind. In this state of readiness, the second and main goal, the reunion of person and kami by means of kami possession, or *kamigakari,* is realized. First she is possessed by the snake responsible for Yoshida-san's affliction and the exorcism is effected. Then, as Satomi-san tells it, she was praying together with the others, when "violent spirit movements suddenly shook my whole body. I charged the kami altar, hopping like a rabbit. I struck the altar—*unh!*—and became still." These "violent spirit movements" are an indication that Satomi-san is being possessed by a kami. With kami possession, the *kishin,* the return of or unification with the kami, is effected.

Here we encounter our second case of human-initiated possession. This time, instead of exorcism, the purpose of the possession is *ukagai:* inquiring of the kami. Satomi-san's teacher and others present ask questions and the kami answers, with Satomi-san serving as the oracle, the mouthpiece of the kami who has possessed her. In the example given, a question is asked concerning the whereabouts of a stolen bicycle, and the kami, through Satomi-san, answers in quite specific terms.

Of her role in this, Satomi-san writes, "Unconsciously, words thrust up in me from the area of the navel. . . . Like a reflex, like an echo, the words flew out." She is here in a state of trance in which the ordinary state of consciousness of the waking self is not engaged. Satomi-san says, "My mind was strained to the point of pain by the sheer not-self." She, as she normally understands herself, is not the one speaking the words in trance; she indicates that when her ordinary state of consciousness intrudes, she is incapable of answering the questions at all. It is only when her ordinary state of consciousness vanishes that the "sheer not-self" allows something to speak through her. What is this which speaks through her? The usual answer is that it is the kami who is speaking through her. For a time, Satomi-san accepts this. Later, however, she develops another idea, one based on Buddhist philosophy.

Buddhist philosophy teaches the existence of what is called the eighth consciousness, a universal consciousness that includes all the individual consciousnesses of every sentient being that has ever lived. In effect, all information, all history, all knowledge is stored there. Satomi-san offers the idea that when she speaks the words of the oracle, she has put aside her normal state of consciousness and tapped into the eighth consciousness. The latter is available to us all, as we are all a part of it, and thus anyone could theoretically do what she does. In practice, though, it is only those who are trained to be able to put aside their ordinary state of consciousness in a controlled manner and at will who are capable of tapping the eighth consciousness in a systematic way. It is significant for Satomi-san's view that one does not feel as if it is oneself speaking in *ukagai.* It is the ordinary state of consciousness that supplies us with our normal sense of self. Since this must be put aside in order to effectively draw on the eighth consciousness, one will inevitably feel that something which is "not self" is speaking. And, in fact, the eighth consciousness is not oneself. Though one is a part of it, it is far greater than oneself alone, for it comprises all sentient beings' consciousnesses, all intelligence; in Buddhist philosophy, it is Mind itself.

This is Satomi-san's idiosyncratic, Buddhist-inspired interpretation of her kami possession experience. How does it compare with the traditional explanation? Ordinarily when one becomes possessed by a kami, the first thing asked is for the kami to identify itself. Then, when someone asks a question such as "Where is my stolen bicycle?," it is that specific kami who answers, through the mouth of the one possessed. Certainly most practitioners would take this response at face value and literally believe that the particular kami named was speaking. In Satomi-san's view, however, this specific kami should be taken as a particular manifestation of the eighth consciousness. Of the snake she has helped exorcise from Yoshida-san, she says, "This was the eighth-consciousness apparition on this occasion." Spirits, kami, and the deceased are all individual manifestations of the universal eighth consciousness. The minds of all sentient beings—which include, for Satomi-san, spirits and kami—are based upon the eighth consciousness; they are like individual waves which are but surface swellings upon the great ocean of Mind, which forms their real substance. If one can put aside the confines of one's own individual mind, then one can sink into the depths of the ocean where all minds meet. By plumbing those depths, one gains access to the mind and identity of every individual—human, kami or spirit. Thus the oracle can speak with the voice and character of the particular kami who has been identified, though the route of access is the eighth consciousness. The medium who puts aside her individual consciousness opens to the universal eighth consciousness and thus becomes a kind of open communication line through which any individual (as a part of the eighth consciousness) may speak.

It should be emphasized that this is not the traditional understanding; it is Satomi-san's individual interpretation. She developed it in response to the dilemma she faced when she converted to Zen: though she felt her experiences in Zen were of greater spiritual value, she nevertheless could not dismiss her earlier experiences with spirits and kami. She was convinced that the spirits she saw were real, the words she spoke as the mouthpiece of the kami were true. She had experienced these things and she could not ignore them, in honesty to herself. Though she turned to Zen and found there the peace and fulfillment that she had sought all her life, she could not put aside her past. Hence, she developed this theory, drawing on elements of Buddhist philosophy to to make her earlier experiences intelligible and philosophically acceptable within the context of her Zen experience and worldview. It is characteristic of Japanese religion and its general (though not universal) climate of religious tolerance that she was able to convert dramatically from one tradition to another without completely repudiating the first. On the contrary, she takes from it what she found there of truth and value and attempts to fit it into her new religious tradition, expanding the latter in the course of her effort.

Mysteries and Marvels

In the world of Japanese religion, the sacred and the mysterious are closely intertwined. This generalization certainly holds true for Satomi-san. We have already seen one instance of this in our discussion of sincerity. Sincerity is a moral and spiritual attitude and mode of behavior that breaks down the barriers between oneself and the sacred world of the kami. It is also power, mysterious spirit power.

Satomi-san's story is primarily that of one in search of the sacred, but it is laced with episodes and incidents concerning the mysterious, the strange, the wonderful, the marvelous. Here is a category of phenomena that includes those things not readily comprehensible by ordinary human reason, that is, the apparently supernatural. Something that is strange or weird, it is felt, most likely has some connection with the world of spirits and kami. Thus the incomprehensible is a wonder, a marvel. Mysteries have an aura of the spiritual, the sacred. This is characteristic of popular Japanese religion in general.

There are many incidents in the text that recount Satomi-san's involvement with "supernatural mysteries." For example, she is initiated into active spiritual life by what she calls a "sacred mystery": a kami speaks to her, telling her to wipe out the evil of the world. This contact with the spirit world is sacred—it starts her on a moral and spiritual quest—and it is a mystery, a secret which she must not betray lest she be doomed to hell.

In the course of Satomi-san's training and functioning as a *miko,* she has many occasions to communicate with the spirits of deceased beings and kami. On one occasion, for example, she was visited, apparently spontaneously, by the spirit of a deceased man who wanted Satomi-san to convey a message to his widow. This supernatural visitation is cause enough for Satomi-san's religious teacher, from whom she was separated at the time, to invite her back for intensive training. In short, by virtue of this supernatural incident, he sees considerable spiritual potential in her.

While studying with her Shinto teacher, Satomi-san is taught a special technique of chanting the Japanese vowel sounds. This practice is unintelligible at face value and requires interpretation in the light of Japanese belief in mysteries. The vowels of the Japanese language are *a, i, u, e, o;* Satomi-san is taught to chant them in scrambled order at the top of her voice and with all the energy in her body. Her teacher heavily stresses the importance of this practice, saying that it is the foundation of her training. Evidently there is something more here than meets the eye.

This "something more" may be traced back to the traditional belief that a supernatural or spiritual power resides in the Japanese language and the sounds that make it up. This belief appears to have been originally an aspect of the general belief that kami reside everywhere, in trees, mountains, the ocean, animals, people, and so forth, and hence in language also. It was believed that not only the words of the kami but also human words had power and could bring acts to realization: with beautiful words one could bring good fortune to another, with terrible words one could inflict harm. Such beliefs lie behind the use of prayers and spells. Even in contemporary works one can find statements asserting, for example, that the words of the Great Purification prayer have "spirit power," and this is why the recitation of the prayer is effective in purifying oneself.[18]

A special variety of the belief that language possesses spirit power is the view that each sound in the Japanese language possesses its own inherent meaning and power, quite distinct from the meaning that people take it to have in ordinary language. This hidden meaning is the true and essential meaning intrinsic to the sound as such since the beginning of time. According to this view, the vowels are especially important; they are the root sources of the universe. When one chants them, one calls up that power which is at the foundation of life itself. By chanting and concentrating on the sounds, one fills one's mind and body with this power, in effect merging with it. The vowels, then, possess extremely potent spirit power, and by chanting them one gains access to that spirit world.[19] It is for this reason that Satomi-san's teacher stresses the importance of this practice.

Satomi-san is initially very much impressed by such mysteries and makes them the focus of her spiritual life. When training to become a *miko,* she lives in expectation of receiving mysterious secrets from her teacher and admires him for the aura of awesome mystery that he bears. On one occasion she asks him about a "marvel" that she had witnessed, a stone statue that was light one moment and heavy the next. When he dismisses this as insignificant, she too quickly loses interest in this particular phenomenon, but then immediately goes on to search for another marvel, another mystery, feeling that in such things something of deep spiritual significance must be hidden.

One of the themes that emerge in Satomi-san's story is her gradual turning away from such marvels and her progressive realization that they are not really what she is interested in, that her spiritual quest actually involves matters of an entirely different order. This realization is slow in coming, however, and painfully acquired. As she says in retrospect, "I thought [satori] was the obtaining of mysterious, esoteric powers." She derides herself for this attitude, saying, "I wandered from the True Way and fell to the level of a mystery monger, chasing vainly after marvels."

In her rejection of mysteries, she reflects the viewpoint of Zen, to which she converted in midlife. She expresses the Zen view when she says of her communication with spirits, "This kind of phenomenon is a by-product of the practice of religion. The main thread of liberation is an entirely different thing." While Zen agrees with the general view in Japanese religion that intensive meditation, fasting, and other religious practices will naturally result in the acquisition of such powers as clair-audience and clairvoyance, orthodox Zen disagrees with the popular view that such powers are desirable, stressing a clear separation between the whole category of mysteries and mar-vels, on the one hand, and true spiritual concerns, on the other. The latter it understands to be only those things which relate to complete freedom from all forms of delusion and suffering. In her search for the Way, Satomi-san gradually learns to distin-guish between these two things.

The New Religions

The New Religions enter into Satomi-san's story only in minor ways, but they are an important part of the overall religious background that generally colors her experience. The New Religions of Japan are a large group of diverse, independent religions numbering in the hundreds. Their individual memberships range from the tens to the millions. Some New Religions have very brief existences; others are over a century old and are still vital in every way.

These religions began to arise at the end of the feudalistic Tokugawa period as a popular response to the degenerate condition of the established religions and the difficult social and economic conditions of the time. Such movements continued to grow and develop during the Meiji and Taishō periods, reflecting continued popular dissatisfaction and unease in the face of the conditions of life and drastic social upheavals the people faced in this period of rapid modernization. Following Japan's defeat in World War II, the New Religions expanded dramatically; again, this should be understood in the context of the despair and bewilderment brought on by defeat, along with the shattered condition of the Japanese economy and social order.

Many different objects of worship and teachings are recognized by the various New Religions; there is no unity among them. Generally, however, these religions attempt to resolve the concrete spiritual and material problems brought to them by members and prospective members, such as questions of finance, health, family relations, and depression. Insofar as they deal with the real problems with which people struggle on an everyday basis, their appeal is very strong.

The religious foundations of the New Religions may be traced to virtually every tradition making up the spectrum of Japanese religions, ancient and modern: Shinto, Buddhism, folk religion, Christianity, and very often amalgams of these. Often the origin of a New Religion lay in the religious experience of its founder (very many of whom were women), usually a person of charismatic or shamanistic nature. Characteristically, the founder had intense and direct personal contact or communication with a kami and on this basis revealed teachings that constituted the doctrine and practice of the New Religion. The founder is usually viewed as either the vessel of the kami, the one in whom the kami resides, or as actively being a kami. Thus the founding person is sacred and holy.

Satomi-san's relationship with the New Religions is largely negative. She is certainly a potential adherent. Faced by personal crisis after crisis, she twice mentions searching among the various religions available to her to find one that could give her what she needed. She is not generally impressed, however, by either the old, established religions or the New Religions. "Most of them," she writes, "were rehashed morality or warmed-over mysteries, or again, a drop of this and a dash of that, offered up in a cocktail. In the end, all they said was that their own sect was right." Thus she finally turns her back on all but Zen.

It is interesting to note that though Satomi-san has a low opinion of the New Religions, her own religious experience and general approach to religion are quite in line with the character of the New Religions phenomenon. She is faced by crises that she feels can only be resolved by religion and engages therefore in a very individualistic religious quest. Intense, personal religious experience becomes the center of her life and the source of meaning in her life; it is the only thing that can give her peace. She is very interested in mysteries, marvels, and the development of spiritual powers. All this is characteristic of those who join New Religions.

Even more striking are the qualities in her religious life that resemble those of the founders of New Religions. She clearly is a shamanistic personality. Many times various kami and spirits speak to her, reveal themselves to her, or possess her, often resulting in insight, revelations, and directives for life that rival in profundity and awesomeness those of many a New Religion. On the other hand, she seems to lack the intense charisma and the organizational skills necessary for the founding and persistence of a religion. In any case, she is clearly not interested. Her mature perspective on such things is given near the end of the text:

> When I think of certain famous persons over whom everyone makes a fuss, such as the founders of certain religions [i.e., the New Religions], I am appalled. When, in their practice of austerities, some abnormal phenomena arise in body or mind, they get carried away. They settle down in this condition and get the idea into their heads that "This is the Supreme Way of Heaven-and-Earth!" There are even cases of people who affect, "In all the universe, I alone am to be revered!" Isn't it really a matter of regret and chagrin that a human being can claim to be the spiritual leader of all existence?

Her rejection of the New Religions here is clearly influenced by Zen. First, she regards intense spiritual practice, especially austerities, as capable of causing apparent "revelations." Second, she does not feel that "revelations" should be taken at face value (though she also does not dismiss them outright; elsewhere she tries to make sense of them in terms of a philosophy acceptable within Zen). Third, she heartily rejects the claims to divinity of these founders, regarding the claims as nothing more than egotism, the worst vice in the Zen view. Fourth and finally, she deplores the power these founders exert over their followers' lives. In addition to the influence of Zen, this passage also shows Satomi-san's own humility, which was thoroughly developed by the time this was written. In sum, it seems that the character of Satomi-san's early religious life and experience was very much consistent with the New Religions, but as this life failed to satisfy her and she turned to Zen, she gradually moved away from this kind of religious life toward one of a very different kind.

Pure Land Buddhism

Pure Land has long been and remains today one of the most popular schools of Buddhism in Japan. This school focuses on the compassionate Buddha Amida and his vows to save humanity from suffering. According to this tradition, the Buddha Amida dwells in the Pure Land, the most blissful paradise of all, to which he wishes to bring all beings. In this happy place, not only is there no suffering, but enlightenment is sure to be attained, since one is there in the company of the Buddha.

The sacred texts of the Pure Land tradition teach that many aeons ago, before he became a buddha, Amida was a bodhisattva named Hōzō (Dharmākara in Sanskrit). At that time he took a number of vows, the most important of which promised that when he became a buddha he would save virtually anyone who reached out to him, by bringing that person to his Pure Land. Of Amida's forty-eight vows, the eighteenth is considered the "Fundamental Vow." In it, the future Amida Buddha vows that he will not become a buddha unless his being a buddha will make it possible for all beings to simply think of him and repeat his name in sincerity ten times and thereby be reborn at death in the Pure Land. Since the Bodhisattva Hōzō did become the Buddha Amida, we are assured that this practice is efficacious. Thus, this vow became the foundation for the practice of the *nembutsu,* the recitation of Buddha Amida's name ("Namu Amida Butsu") as a religious practice.

Worship of Amida Buddha and the invocation of the *nembutsu* were first popularized in Japan during the Kamakura period (1185–1333). In this period, many Japanese were convinced that they were living in the age of *mappō,* the age of the "degenerate Dharma," during which time, it was said, humanity's abilities had degenerated so much since the time of the Buddha that people were no longer capable of practicing the "heroic" path of "self-power" taught in traditional Buddhism. That is, they were no longer capable of reaching enlightenment by their own efforts through such traditional Buddhist practices as morality and meditation. In step with this widespread view, several paths were popularized that were claimed to be "easier" and hence more appropriate for the time. One of these was Pure Land Buddhism. In this tradition, one does not try to seek enlightenment by "self-power" but instead relies on the "Other-power" of a perfectly enlightened and infinitely compassionate being, Amida Buddha. Thus, the Pure Land Buddhist gives up a self-reliance that demands the impossible and turns in humility and faith to a being who truly does possess the ability to liberate perplexed humanity from delusion and suffering. This is a path that is straightforward and secure to the Pure Land faithful.

Satomi-san's encounter with Pure Land Buddhism is discussed in relatively brief terms in her account. She indicates that while she found Pure Land very emotionally satisfying, this form of Buddhism left her with certain philosophical problems that she could not resolve. She says that "talks on Amida Buddha's Fundamental Vow always led me into a state of happy intoxication," and it is small wonder that she felt this way. After years of earnest effort on the path of "self-power," she felt no closer to a resolution of her spiritual malaise than she had before she began. What a relief, and how thrilling, to hear that one could acknowledge one's incapacity for the struggle and leave everything up to a supreme being. And yet she was stumped. The Pure Land sect into which she had wandered stressed the immensity of the qualitative gulf between the delusion and evil of humanity and the perfection of Amida. Thus the reliance on the "Other-power" of Amida was quite absolute. Yet the Pure Land tradition also indicates that though Amida is constantly sending waves of compassion out toward humanity (just as the sun constantly beams out light), humanity must do its part. A person must respond to Amida's compassion, must give up self-effort and turn to Amida in humility and faith. Thus salvation is after all, in this sense, mutual. Satomi-san's puzzle hinges on this mutuality—what is an individual's role in salvation? If we are so utterly lowly, how can we ever expect to do our part to enter into this relationship of faith? There are answers to these questions in the Pure Land tradition, but they are subtle, and Satomi-san evidently failed to find satisfaction in them.

One suspects, on the basis of what transpires in the rest of the text, that in the end Satomi-san simply could not accept the Pure Land view of human nature. Though she was highly self-critical and quite ready to label herself stupid or immoral, she was also strongly inclined toward independence and self-effort. Though she felt she was constantly failing to measure up to the standards she set for herself, and ever disappointed in her behavior and meager spiritual attainments, she always hoped for better from herself and worked incessantly at self-improvement. Thus her turn toward Zen, with its view of human nature, brought her at last to her spiritual home. In Zen, the behavior of the ordinary, unenlightened person is deprecated as utterly deluded and harmful, yet at the same time human nature as such is lauded as intrinsically enlightened. Thus it is stressed that there is great potential for moral and wise behavior in every individual, this potential making the shabby comportment of most people all the more regrettable. Zen advocates hard work to realize this potential. This perspective suited Satomi-san well.

Zen Buddhism

Zen (Chinese: Ch'an) Buddhism is a school of Buddhism which originated in China, where imported Indian Buddhist ideas and practices mingled with Chinese culture, especially Taoism, to produce something new. Zen was introduced into Japan in the twelfth and thirteenth centuries and, finding favor with the samurai rulers of the country, artists, and spiritual seekers, underwent further development there.

Zen is the Japanese pronunciation of the Sanskrit *dhyāna,* "meditation." Though meditation is important in many Buddhist schools, Zen relies on it to a degree and with an exclusivity not seen elsewhere. Meditation is the beginning and end of Zen practice. *Zazen,* or seated meditation, is the basic form of meditation practice in Zen (a synonym for "meditation" in Zen is "sitting"). Basically, it involves meditating while sitting on the floor in one of a number of possible postures, including the Japanese posture, *seiza* (sitting on one's knees with back straight, weight resting on the lower legs and feet), the full lotus posture (sitting on one's buttocks with straight back, legs crossed, feet on thighs, and knees on floor), and the half-lotus posture (the same but with the left foot on the right thigh and the right foot under the left thigh). In all postures, the eyes are open but cast down in a restful position, and the hands are brought together in the lap with the left hand resting lightly in the right hand and thumbs touching, forming a circle with thumbs and fingers.

The meditation practice itself varies with teacher, practitioner and Zen sect, but I shall mention some of the most common. A practice frequently assigned to beginners, but also used in a variant form by more advanced meditators, is the counting of the breath. One breathes naturally but slowly through the nose, counting "one" for the inhalation, "two" for the exhalation, "three" for the next inhalation, and so forth up to ten, all the while attempting to concentrate one's mind fully on this process of counting breaths. When one reaches ten, one starts over, repeating the practice until the meditation period is over (a typical meditation round may last twenty-five to forty minutes). No attempt is made to slow or stop the breath artificially, though as the meditation deepens, the breathing will slow naturally. A somewhat more advanced form of this practice is to give up the counting and concentrate the mind on the breathing itself.

A second practice of interest is called *shikan-taza,* or "just sitting." The "just" is deceptive; this is not a practice of sitting aimlessly to pass the time doing nothing, the mind wandering about randomly. Rather, in *shikan-taza* one hopes to concentrate the mind entirely upon the mind itself. Yet the sitting is done purposelessly in a sense; the desirable state is one in which the mind is simply "there," clear, fully alert, calm, and yet energetic. There is nothing outside of oneself that one wants to attain or realize; the point is to let the process of mentation be what it is naturally and to see that clearly. This is a rather difficult practice, as there are no artificial devices such as words or numbers on which to concentrate; one must simply be in a state of concentration, without concentrating on anything in particular at all.

A final practice that must be mentioned is kōan practice. The kōan is a tool developed in Zen for meditation. It is, in effect, a puzzle that the student must solve, though there is no set answer to it. It cannot be resolved by the use of ordinary reason or logic but only by calling on mental skills that, Zen claims, we all possess but rarely use. It is the aim of Zen to awaken such neglected mental abilities. A kōan is a statement, question, or dialogue that is fundamentally nonlogical or paradoxical in nature. Thus, to see through the kōan, one must use mental abilities that are not based on logic. For example, a famous kōan developed by Hakuin is, "What is the sound of one hand clapping?" There is clearly no logical answer to such a question, but when a Zen master assigns this kōan, the student must nonetheless come up with an answer. Hence the student must learn to use the mind in new ways.

One kōan that calls for special comment is the kōan "Mu." Satomi-san works with and speaks of this kōan extensively in the text, and it is, in any case, probably the most famous and widely used of all the kōans. It reads as follows, "A monk once asked Master Joshu, 'Has a dog the Buddha Nature or not?' Joshu said, 'Mu!'"[20] Jōshu here is the Zen master; the monk is his disciple. In inquiring about Buddha nature, the monk raises a point in Buddhist philosophy that must detain us a while, as it is crucial not only to this kōan, but to Satomi-san's story and to Zen practice in general.

Zen emphasizes that all sentient beings, all beings with intelligence, possess Buddha nature.[21] This means that all possess the potential to become a buddha, an enlightened being. It must be emphasized, however, that the Buddha nature is not a "thing," a self, soul, or essence that we possess. All schools of Buddhism deny the existence in human beings of a permanent unchanging self or soul, and Zen strongly emphasizes this as one of the foundations of its teaching. It is taught that we do not possess a self because we, and everything about us, are constantly changing. To exist is to exist in time, to become what we are from moment to moment, not to "be" a static entity. Thus, one crucial aspect of enlightenment in Zen is to become free of attachment to the idea that we possess a self or soul, to realize that the essence of the human being is fundamentally not of the nature of a self. In Buddhist language, we are "not-self." To realize "not-self" is to realize what one ultimately is, to answer the question "Who or what am I?" For one can only free oneself of the delusion of belief in self by realizing what the true nature of one's being is.

Of course, to say that we are "not-self" is to put the matter negatively. To say the same thing in positive language, Buddhists identify the true nature of our being with "Buddha nature." It was stated above that Buddha nature is our potential to become a buddha, but now it must be added that from another perspective, it is also the case that we already are buddhas; that is, our true nature is that of an enlightened being. Basically, this means that although we ordinarily appear to ourselves to be confused, deluded, and egocentric beings, by virtue of the fact that we are born as sentient beings, these qualities are not intrinsic to human nature nor is it inevitable that we behave in this manner. Human nature is intrinsically good; sentience or awareness is inherently enlightened. The mind, by virtue of what it is, naturally functions to see clearly, to know. However, because of old habits and prejudices that the human race has maintained since time immemorial, all human beings have, in effect, lost touch with this basic enlightened nature that is their birthright. Instead of behaving like enlightened beings, we behave selfishly, with anger, jealousy, pride, ignorance, envy, possessiveness, and all the other vices with which we are all too familiar. Our ignorant habits have become so deeply engrained and familiar that we have come to take them as our true nature; the idea that we are really buddhas is so far out of touch with our experience of ourselves and our knowledge of human history that it seems impossible. Yet Zen insists that we can discover the truth of this claim by practicing Zen, which will enable us to see for ourselves, in direct, personal experience, the truth of this statement. Hence, the basic Zen position on human nature and human potential is radically optimistic: you are buddha, you are a perfectly enlightened being, it claims. However, you must practice Zen meditation in order to realize this truth.

Why must one practice if one already is buddha? You already are buddha, says Zen, but to hear or read these words is far from sufficient. If one does not personally experience this buddhahood, one's enlightened nature will remain concealed by aeons of bad habits and delusion, staying out of sight and out of mind—out of the reach of our conscious personality, which we, in our delusion, identify with "ourself." With this in mind, Zen Buddhists distinguish between "original" and "acquired" enlightenment. The former is Buddha nature, the enlightened nature that is inherent to all sentient beings. The latter is that same Buddha nature after we have practiced Zen and experienced enlightenment, becoming aware of the enlightenment that was always ours.

To be free of delusion—all delusion whatsoever concerning oneself, others, life—is to be enlightened. In other words, since we already are enlightened beings by nature, since the mind is itself enlightenment, enlightenment is not something that we have to acquire. It is not something outside of or beyond us; it *is* us, the true nature of our being. Hence, if we can put aside our delusion, even for a moment, our enlightened nature will shine forth of its own accord. This is difficult, of course, and ordinarily takes years of Zen practice, for old, deeply engrained habits are not easily broken. Yet many a Zen practitioner who "breaks through" to enlightenment exclaims, "It was right before me all along!"

Enlightenment in Zen has many names and synonyms, each expressive of a different aspect of enlightenment. There are two basic Japanese terms, often used interchangeably, though sometimes it is important to distinguish between them. *Kenshō* means seeing the self, that is, the true self or Buddha nature. The phrase "true self" is interesting since Buddhists, including Zen Buddhists, deny the existence of a self. The true self of Zen, it must be emphasized, is not an eternal, unchanging self or soul. It is identical with not-self and Buddha nature; it is what one sees when one becomes free of all the ideas one acquires about what one is. It is the true nature of one's being, but, unlike a soul, it is not attached to "me" alone, nor is it "mine." My true self is another's true self and ultimately the true nature of all existents and of existence or life itself. To see this is *kenshō,* perhaps best translated as "self-realization."

Satori is enlightenment, experiential knowledge of Truth or Reality. It is often used interchangeably with *kenshō,* but the two terms are sometimes distinguished by the connotation of greater depth attached to satori. *Kenshō* may be used to refer to first enlightenment, whether a relatively shallow glimpse or a deeper realization. Satomi-san says of herself that she has experienced a preliminary *kenshō.* Satori, when it is distinguished from *kenshō,* refers to deep realization.

Realization, awakening, and *liberation* are other English words used to refer to enlightenment. *Realization* emphasizes the experiential aspect of enlightenment; one "makes real" in one's experience what one has heard or been taught about Buddha nature, not-self, and so on; one "makes real" for oneself the Buddha nature, which has always been present but outside of experience. *Awakening* emphasizes the idea that our ordinary state of consciousness, far from being the norm with which we should identify ourselves and which we should consider to be reality, is like a state of sleep, in that we use only a fraction of the mental power which is ours, or like a dream, in that we are confused by images and experience that we misunderstand. In our ordinary state of consciousness, we take our misinterpretation of reality for reality; when enlightened, we see truly for the first time, the dimly perceived becomes clear, the apparition is seen through and dismissed, and a new sense of vigor and clarity is ours. Finally, *liberation* connotes freedom from unhappiness and suffering. The enlightened are not emotionless automatons. They feel the same sensations as anyone, the same joy, love, compassion, and other emotions. The difference is that the emotional life of the enlightened is said to be free of selfishness. Hence, for example, there is no fear of death. If sick, they feel the sensations of the disease, but without self-pity or self-indulgence. Whatever life brings is accepted for what it is, neither more nor less. There is no stress, no tension. The liberated is freed from the cares of life, not in turning away from them, but in seeing deeply into them.

With this background, let us return to the kōan Mu. When the monk asks whether a dog has Buddha nature, the Zen master does not give what we might consider a straightforward answer; he does not say yes or no. Indeed, how could he? For we have seen that the Buddha nature is not something that a dog or a person "has." Insofar as Buddha nature is the true nature of life itself, it encompasses both having and not having, being and not being.[22] It is a single reality that encompasses both these poles, though the rational mind can only think of having and not having, being and not being, as mutually exclusive opposites. The master's cry of "Mu!" (which literally means "No!") does not mean that the dog has no Buddha nature. It is a negation of the question itself and of the whole condition of mind that could produce such a question. It also expresses Buddha nature by speaking from an awareness that knows the way in which having and not having are not different. "Mu" embodies this nondifferentiation. To meditate on this kōan, one must try to utterly penetrate to the bottom of this Mu, this negation of both having and not having, being and not being. Only a mind that is not operating in terms of the two poles of this dualism can resolve this kōan satisfactorily. This is the mind of Buddha nature. If Buddha nature speaks to the Zen master, the kōan is passed; if the ordinary mind speaks, the kōan remains unresolved.

Kōans are tools that are used initially to help the student break through to enlightenment and later to probe different aspects of enlightenment, thereby deepening the enlightenment. Of the two major Zen sects in Japan, the Rinzai sect is known for the use of kōans. The other major sect, Sōtō, is known for eschewing the use of kōans and emphasizing *shikan-taza*, "just sitting." These differences reflect other differences in philosophy and style between the two sects. Rinzai proponents feel that the Sōtō emphasis on *shikan-taza* promotes quietism and withdrawal, attitudes that are antithetical to the Zen insistence on active engagement in everyday life. Sōtō, for its part, feels that the Rinzai use of kōans encourages the practitioner to fixate on enlightenment as something to be attained, thus nurturing attitudes of desire (for enlightenment) and acquisitiveness, which bolster the ego and its demands— precisely the opposite effect to what one wishes in Zen. Sōtō proponents feel *shikan-taza* allows the ego to die a natural death, as the enlightened mind of Buddha nature shines out ever more clearly.

Satomi-san studied with a Zen master, Yasutani Hakuun, who, though a teacher in the Sōtō Zen sect, combined the methods of Rinzai and Sōtō, insisting that both are necessary to the Zen practitioner. He assigned his students whatever meditation practice he felt best suited their character, aspiration, and level of advancement, whether it was counting the breath, *shikan-taza,* or a kōan. In this he followed his teacher, Harada Sogaku.[23]

Though Yasutani Rōshi assigned his students a variety of meditation practices in accordance with what seemed to suit the various individuals best, he felt strongly enough about kōans that he considered them an essential part of Zen training. Students who completed their training under Yasutani Rōshi were required to work through 546 koans.[24] In some cases, it might take years to work through a single kōan; others might be resolved within hours. Nonetheless, it is clear that a complete course of Zen training is not a thing to be undertaken casually. It always requires years of training, involving a determined and self-disciplined effort on the part of the student. Satomi-san was more than willing to face this challenge. After a lifetime of seeking, she found in Zen her final spiritual home.

Notes for Part Two

1. The words of Emperor Meiji, 30 November 1868, 3 February 1870, and 3 February 1870, respectively. Cited in Shōzō Kōno, "Kannagara no Michi," *Monumenta Nipponica* 3 (1940): 385.

2. Masaharu Anesaki, *Religious Life of the Japanese People: Its Present Status and Historical Background* (Tokyo: Kokusai Bunka Shinkokai, 1938), p. 31. It should be noted that in the 1961 revised version of this book there are substantial revisions in the section on Kannagara-no-Michi.

3. Sokyo Ono, in collaboration with William P. Woodard, *Shinto: The Kami Way* (Tokyo and Rutland, Vt.: Charles Tuttle Co., 1962), p. 8.

4. Yamakage Motohisa, *Shintō Nyūmon,* vol. 2: *Gyōbōhen* (Tokyo: Hakuba Shuppan, 1982), p. 68.

5. Wing-tsit Chan, trans., in *A Source Book in Chinese Philosophy* (Princeton: Princeton University Press, 1963), pp. 107–108.

6. Sugawara-no-Michizane (845–903) was a famous scholar and politician who was unjustly exiled to Kyūshū, where he died. His angry spirit was said to have taken revenge on the emperor and several court officials, so in order to appease him he was enshrined as a kami at the Kitano Jinja in Kyoto, a very popular shrine to this day. The poem is cited in Ono Sokyo, "Makoto," in *Shintō Jiten,* ed. Yasuzu and Umeda (Osaka: Horishōten, 1938), p. 560f.

7. Ibid., p. 561. The emperor was, of course, regarded as a living kami.

8. Cited by Joseph J. Spae, *Japanese Religiosity* (Tokyo: Oriens Institute for Religious Research, 1971), p. 109.

9. Yamakage, p. 68.

10. Cf. Donald Philippi, *Norito: A New Translation of the Ancient Japanese Ritual Prayers* (Tokyo: Institute for Japanese Culture and Classics, Kokugaku University, 1959), pp. 45–49.

11. Carmen Blacker, *The Catalpa Bow: A Study of Shamanistic Practices in Japan* (London: George Allen and Unwin, 1975), p. 85.

12. Carmen Blacker (p. 92) notes that many others suffer physically from such efforts.
13. In her excellent study, Carmen Blacker notes that she found no evidence of breathing techniques in the Japanese shamanistic tradition (of which *miko* such as Satomi-san are a part). But Satomi-san is taught such techniques as essential to her training. Cf. Blacker, p. 98.
14. Cited in Ichiro Hori, *Folk Religion in Japan: Continuity and Change* (Chicago: University of Chicago Press, 1968), p. 187.
15. Cf. Donald Philippi, trans., *Kojiki* (Princeton: Princeton University Press, 1969), chaps. 92 and 93.
16. Mircea Eliade, *Shamanism: Archaic Techniques of Ecstasy,* trans. Willard R. Trask, Bollingen Series 76 (Princeton: Princeton University Press, 1964), chaps. 6–7, 9, 12 passim.
17. The topic of sexism in institutional Shinto and Buddhism is far too complex to be adequately treated here. Briefly, insofar as Shinto and Buddhism belong to the great tradition and possess a formally institutionalized priesthood, the public leadership of these religions has, of course, been overwhelmingly male-dominated, though women were admitted to the Shinto priesthood in 1945. Moreover, with respect to restrictions on the ordinary female religious practitioner, in Shinto women during their menstrual periods were traditionally banned from visiting Shinto shrines because of a taboo on flowing blood. In Buddhism, monasticism was in many respects deleterious to the full participation of women. For example, women were forbidden access to many holy places in Japan, including the sacred mountains, Mount Hiei and Mount Koya, the respective headquarters of the Tendai and Shingon sects of Buddhism, which were reserved for monks. Dōgen Zenji, the preeminent Zen Rōshi and philosopher, argued forcefully for the mundane and spiritual equality of women and while teaching just outside the city of Kyoto opened his community to everyone, including women. However, when he later founded the temple, Eiheiji, and moved to a remote mountain area, access to his teachings was again largely restricted to the male monastic community. (On Dōgen, cf. Deborah Hopkinson, "Women and Kamakura Buddhism: Dōgen," in *Kahawai: Journal of Women and Zen* 1, nos. 1, 2, 3, Winter, Spring, Summer 1979.) Of course, Shinto and Zen are far from exceptional in this regard; all the great institutional forms of religion are sexist in major ways.

The reader is referred, for Buddhism, to I. B. Horner, *Women under*

Primitive Buddhism (Delhi: Motilal Banarsidass, 1975); Diana Y. Paul, *Women in Buddhism* (Berkeley: Asian Humanities Press, 1979); and *Kahawai: Journal of Women and Zen* (Diamond Sangha, 2119 Kaloa Way, Honolulu, HI 96822). For Shinto, see Karen A. Smyers, "Women and Shinto: The Relation between Purity and Pollution," *Japanese Religions* 12 (July 1983): 7–18; and Haruko Okano, *Die Stellung der Frau in Shintō* (Wiesbaden: Otto Harrassowitz, 1976). A rewarding volume dedicated to the subject "Women and Religion in Japan" is *Japanese Journal of Religious Studies* 10 (June–September 1983).

18. Yamakage, p. 42. This author specifically urges the chanting of the five vowels for their spirit power.

19. Such ideas are taught by many of the later Kokugaku (National Learning) thinkers. Kannagara-no-Michi, as we have seen, is one variety of Kokugaku.

20. Zenkei Shibayama, *Zen Comments on the Mumonkan,* trans. Sumiko Kudo (New York: New American Library, 1974), p. 19.

21. There is a closely related teaching that all things, animate and inanimate, *are* Buddha nature. This teaching is touched upon in the discussion of *kenshō* below. Regarding the present teaching that all sentient beings possess Buddha nature, it should be noted that this refers to all who wander in the six births, i.e., beings in hell, hungry ghosts, animals, fighting demons, human beings, and heavenly beings.

22. Cf. Yasutani Rōshi's commentary on Mu, translated in Philip Kapleau, *The Three Pillars of Zen,* rev. ed. (Garden City, N.Y.: Doubleday/Anchor Press, 1980), p. 76.

23. This line is represented in America by two well-known and highly respected Zen masters, Roshi Philip Kapleau of Rochester, New York and Santa Fe, New Mexico, and Roshi Robert Aitken of Honolulu, Hawaii, both of whom studied Zen under Yasutani Rōshi.

24. Kapleau, p. 370.

Bibliography

This bibliography lists sources available in English for the reader interested in further pursuing the ideas and practices discussed in this book. I have stressed materials on Shinto and popular Japanese religion since these traditions are less well known in the United States and resources on them are more difficult to find. As books on Zen are readily available, references to Zen are limited to two books that directly treat material involved in Satomi-san's Zen practice. Kapleau translates into English lectures by Yasutani Rōshi, and Shibayama presents and discusses the kōans with which Satomi-san worked.

In addition, I would like to refer interested readers to two remembrances of Satomi-san that have been published in *Kahawai: Journal of Women and Zen* 2 (Winter 1980). This very interesting journal, published by a lay Zen group, may be ordered from Diamond Sangha, 2119 Kaloa Way, Honolulu, HI 96822.

BIBLIOGRAPHY

Anesaki, Masaharu. *Religious Life of the Japanese People: Its Present Status and Historical Background.* Tokyo: Kokusai Bunka Shinkokai, 1938.

Blacker, Carmen. *The Catalpa Bow: A Study of Shamanistic Practices in Japan.* London: George Allen and Unwin, 1975.

Davis, Winston. *Dojo: Magic and Exorcism in Modern Japan.* Stanford: Stanford University Press, 1980.

Eliade, Mircea. *Shamanism: Archaic Techniques of Ecstasy.* Translated by Willard R. Trask. Bollingen Series 76. Princeton, N.J.: Princeton University Press, 1964.

~ BIBLIOGRAPHY ~

Fairchild, William P. "Shamanism in Japan." *Folklore Studies* 21 (1961): 1–122.

Fane, Richard Ponsonby. *The Vicissitudes of Shinto.* Dr. Richard Ponsonby Fane Series 5. Kyoto: Ponsonby Memorial Society, 1963.

Hori, Ichiro. *Folk Religion in Japan: Continuity and Change.* Edited by Joseph M. Kitagawa and Alan L. Miller. Chicago: University of Chicago Press, 1968.

Kapleau, Philip. *The Three Pillars of Zen.* Rev. ed. New York: Anchor Books, 1980.

Kishimoto, Hideo, ed. *Japanese Religion in the Meiji Era.* Translated by John F. Howes. Japanese Culture in the Meiji Era 2: Religion. Tokyo: Ōbunsha, 1956.

Kōno, Shōzō. "Kannagara no Michi." *Monumenta Nipponica* 3 (1940): 369–391.

Lowell, Percival. *Occult Japan or The Way of the Gods: An Esoteric Study of Japanese Personality and Possession.* Boston: Houghton Mifflin, 1895.

Murakami, Shigeyoshi. *Japanese Religion in the Modern Century.* Translated by H. Byron Earhart. Tokyo: University of Tokyo Press, 1980.

Ono, Sokyo. *Shinto: The Kami Way.* In collaboration with William P. Woodard. Rutland, Vt.: Charles Tuttle Co., 1962.

Ross, Floyd Hiatt. *Shinto: The Way of Japan.* Boston: Beacon Press, 1965.

Shibayama, Zenkei. *Zen Comments on the Mumonkan.* Translated by Sumiko Kudo. New York: Harper and Row, 1974; reprint ed., Mentor Books.

Spae, Joseph J. *Japanese Religiosity.* Tokyo: Oriens Institute for Religious Research, 1971.

———. *Shinto Man.* Tokyo: Oriens Institute for Religious Research, 1972.